Kim,

Jone never
Never give up
believe in your ten
Jone and blessings
Jone Karen Bode

CLEAN HEART
Healing Body, Soul and Spirit

Though one may be overpowered by another,
two can withstand them.
And a threefold cord is not quickly broken.
(Ecclesiastes 4:12)

Karen, Kyloon and Me

DEDICATION

I happily dedicate this book to my daughters and grandchildren, present and future. I love them all from the moon and back.

This book is also dedicated to all of God's powerful women, who are searching for a purity and humbleness of hearts, once experienced as a child. Also, I dedicate this book to all women who have made a promise to make a commitment, be consistent, have courage, and most of all, be in constant communication with one another, while seeking a closer relationship with God.

FOREWORD

*A*t times, tears were welling up in my eyes, partly because of my personal knowledge of things that went on in your life, but mostly because I can identify with your journey, both person-ally and professionally. It is a story of healing that people need to hear. As a pastoral counselor, I often would like to have people read and hear that they [can] find victory and peace with God, self, and others. Thank you for your courage, and may God continue to bless you. Let's keep in touch.

Your brother in Christ,
Alan Wohlander

I attended Karen Bode's class and read her book, "CleanHeart". This book inspired me to be so much more of my authentic self. I learned to love myself and accept God's love in a way that I had never experienced before. Throughout each class, I had to inspect my heart and pull from within all the painful things that I had buried for so long. I had to accept these things and let them go. I had to learn that these things were not from God and that we are love. God loves ME!!!!!! We read over and over again how God loves us and I was able to give God all my hurts and through this class fellowship, I learned that I was not the only one hurting and that there is nothing wrong with me. I learned that I am perfectly, fearfully made!! I learned for the first time who I am in God and where I am with God in His eyes. I learned that it is through God's mercy and grace that I finally learned how to love myself. Although I am still a work in progress, I would not be where I am today if it wasn't for her book, insights and suggested questions at each end of the chapters. I learned how to clean out my heart just as Karen did. As there are multiple parts/layers to each individual person that makes us who we are, I found a lot of similarities with Karen, the young girl and Kyloon, the survivor. I am in the process of becoming, "Me, as Karen had experienced in her journey....I am so grateful to have had the blessing of reading her journey and inspiring me to grow and love, rather than be a victim of society/hurts I was becoming. I am letting go of some of what I have endured. During this class, I have written specifically what I want for goals for my life and my visions, as they come to me. I now am walking and growing with God. I, no doubt, would not be where I am without God leading me to this fantastic group of women to help me get out of the place I was trapped in. Karen's book, "CleanHeart" has been instrumental in my relationship in knowing God and His love for me and my family.

Cassie
Rockland, Maine July 2015

For a personal consultation on how Karen can help you, your loved ones, or your group, contact Karen at www.thepowerfulwomenofgod.org and please leave a brief description of your request or need. Messages will be answered within a few days. She honors each and every request with prayers while anticipating God's blessings on each.

TABLE OF CONTENTS

WHAT I WANT IN LIFE

- To be content with myself
- To make decisions on my own
- To be confident with my decisions and their consequences
- To believe in myself
- To allow myself to make mistakes and not crucify myself
- To move in nature's circle and let it occur without criticism from myself
- To make friends and believe myself worthy of their friendship
- To not think that I am not good enough
- To be a positive role model for my daughters
- To leave this pain behind me once and for all
- To know that I am loved

Dear God,

Why am I having such a problem with all this? I've lived too long under the premise that I was not good enough. Circumstances will prove that we all fall short in life, but whose life does not? Why do I take it to such extremes? Living under an abusive relationship does confirm such a belief. Life's experiences will also confirm this, but why does my mind? I have the choice. I don't have to go there now, but I do. Why? I want to change. I understand the mind and how it works, but I can't. Why? Am I depressed? Do I not have control of my mind? God, I ask you to intervene! Help me, when I cannot.

-Karen

(This is a prayer of desperation I wrote on October 31, 2008.)

INTRODUCTION

"Some people think that holding on tight makes one strong, but sometimes, it's the letting go." — Unknown

For our struggle is not against flesh and blood, but against the rulers, against the authorities, against the powers of this dark world and against the spiritual forces of evil in the heavenly realms.
(Ephesians 6:12 NIV)

Have you ever thought that you were beyond repair?
Have you ever been reduced to feelings of unworthiness, helplessness, and brokenness?
Have you ever felt suicide was the only way of escape from your own internal negative voices?

Well, Karen, Kyloon, and Me, the authors of this book, want to tell you their story of how they were held captive by just such "emotional monsters." We want to share with you how we found our way through a long and arduous journey, only to discover the hidden and lost parts of our collective soul. Ultimately, you will see we found freedom from self-hatred and rediscovered self-love.

My real name is Karen, but I want you, the reader, to know why I wrote in the third person as, Kyloon. She is very much a part of me. If it had not been for Kyloon, I would not be telling this story. It was because of her courage and desire to be heard that I am able to tell you the rest of the story. Karen has been living in shame, fear, and with all the other monsters mentioned above for too long.

My dream is to have a life I can be proud of.

The reason I started to write this story as Kyloon was because it was much easier to tell a story about another person rather than take ownership of what truly happened to me. As my story proceeded and took form, I began to understand that Kyloon was not, of course, another person, but another entity within me who wanted to tell her story. I used Kyloon because it was the name a Chinese Christian man I knew in Ecuador used to call me with adoration and affection. It was at that time, I learned to truly love myself with my whole heart. To me, the name, Kyloon, means love, honor, and respect.

So, here is the story of Karen—*my story*—of recovery.

As we begin, I want you to know that no matter how broken your body, soul, or spirit is, there is a wonderful and beautiful future for you. You truly are able to live and feel your soul soar, your body thrive, and your spirit sing with peace, love, and joy. However, to experience these positive areas in life, you must be willing to face your own personal "monsters" and release them to God.

What are these monsters?

They are spiritual holdings that exist to kill and destroy all the happiness, joy, and love that you might otherwise experience. You are in a warfare that is not readily visible in this world, but it is very real. The only lasting way to set yourself free from these emotional "monsters" is to expose the true nature. By identifying and exposing these "monsters," you open the window of your heart to God and allow Him to disengage their destructive hold on your life.

This story is about me, a middle-aged woman, who had been held captive by these "monsters" for most of her life. Through the determination and love of her "survivor self," Kyloon, she was able to expose the truth concerning her own internal struggle. Many generational chains, that had caused her and her family turmoil, were revealed and broken. Once they were exposed and broken, Karen, was able to find the child lost within her soul, who had been locked up for forty-one years. She accomplished the healing of her body, soul, and spirit with a single prayer spoken to God each morning:

> **"Lord, create in me a clean heart,**
> **so that I might be of service to You."**

CHAPTER 1

GROWING UP

Facing the Monsters

One night, as Kyloon was alone in her house, she wrote down her thoughts in a journal, hoping it might help her better understand what had happened the previous week. Her thoughts were causing her nightmares, so she reasoned babbling on a piece of paper might help her explain how and why she came face to face with her many "monsters."

Kyloon had recently moved to her new home in New England and had been crazy busy all week, desperately trying to get ready for her first day of school. She had unpacked all the boxes, and gotten her children settled in their new schools. Then she discovered something was terribly wrong. Instead of getting ready for the new day, she was suddenly contemplating suicide as an alternative to living there with her husband. Kyloon was in trouble and she knew it.

Without a second thought, Kyloon went to God and prayed.

God answered her prayer by saying, "I want all of you: heart and soul."

I'm not sure I can do that, she thought. *I have been hiding for so long. Can I really strip down and be emotionally exposed? What is the alternative? Do I want to live with the reality that suicide is a viable choice?*

She quickly decided on the former.

Then the accusing, mocking voice pounded in her head, "You are just a coward!"

"I am not a coward!" she screamed back.

A very persistent and quiet voice nudged the inner core of her being and said repeatedly, "Change, change, change."

She decided her only option was to open up completely to God, ask for His help, and follow His plan. She knew she didn't have the courage or strength to change on her own.

That's when her daily morning prayer became, "Create in me a clean heart, Lord, so that I may be of service to You."

The Child

My mom and dad began dating in their junior year of high school and promptly decided to marry the year after graduation. Dad was being shipped to Bremen, Germany, and separation was not an option for them. My mom went to Germany as his wife. Little did they know that their choice to stay together would carry through to their last few days of life on earth—in the same hospital in Worcester, Massachusetts. As they had started together, so they remained together until my mother passed away in February of 2007. They had chosen to stay as one, despite their challenges, even to their deaths.

Seven years after my parents returned from Germany, my older sister was born. I came next, two and a half years later. Although from the same parents, we couldn't have been more different. My sister was an obedient child who always followed the rules without question. While she sat in the corner reading her book, my time was spent in much more active, festive activities. I ran naked to our neighborhood store at the age of three. My younger sister was born ten years after me. To my parent's delight, she, too, was a quiet and sweet baby, unlike their middle child, me.

Yes, I was adventurous, to say the least. I wanted to know how and why things worked. I wanted to run, see, and do things. I wanted to feel free. I loved the outdoors. Life was a mystery that I wanted to figure out.

Included in our immediate family was my father's mother. Both my grandparents from my mother's side had died before I was born. My father's mother, Grammy, was a bit eccentric. She lived upstairs in our house and was an artist type and a musician. She taught music to many neighborhood students—including my sisters and me. She was a divorced woman, which was unusual for those times, and had raised my father on her own just a short way from where we now lived. I remember her as a little strange and aloof—she never fit into the box that I was trying to fit her into: "normalcy." She read Tarot cards—but always behind the closed doors of her bedroom.

In our living room, we had a beautiful baby grand piano—it took up almost half of the room. It was a dark cedar red color. I remember the color because one of my chores was to polish the piano when guests came to the house, which was often. The only time Grammy would come downstairs was to teach us piano. It was expected that we would all take music lessons until we were teenagers—then we could decide for ourselves if music was in our futures.

Playing piano and violin were not natural for me, but as my father's daughter—I had no choice. I did, however, like the performing end of it because of the attention it brought, but I didn't like practicing.

The house was full of music—bands playing, piano playing, or singing. Dad was a music teacher, taught lessons on the side, and was always practicing with the band. A second generation Swede played the drums and guitar in my dad's band. He was an out-of-the-box thinker, and we spent hours talking philosophical issues of life when he wasn't practicing with my dad. I always liked that!

Some of my fondest memories are of the two Christmas caroling parties we had at in our house, one with the professional musicians and the other with all our friends and family. Before the evening was done, the house would be filled with people eating, drinking, and laughing around our baby grand piano—the one I had polished and wiped down until it shown brightly.

Music was also the only thing that connected my father and me. I was afraid of him. He criticized my music. Nothing was good enough; I never got praise from him. No matter how hard I tried, he always found something wrong with it. He didn't like the pitch, the tone, or that band I liked. I simply wasn't good enough. Secretly, my heart was searching for acceptance from my father, which I felt I could never achieve.

When I was growing up, I always felt that I let my parents down because I was not quiet or happy sitting and reading a book. Actually, that was the last thing I wanted to do. Words just didn't make sense to me. I struggled with reading, and remember to this day the reading program they put me in in third grade. I hated that stupid program because I felt that I couldn't make adequate progress. Nevertheless, I learned to fake my reading ability or just cover up my inability to learn. That was not a difficult task because verbally, I was really smart. Learning and struggling went hand in hand during my early childhood. Later on in life, I found out that I'd had a learning disability during my childhood that had never been diagnosed. Now, I finally understand why learning was so difficult for me in my early years.

However, cooking was different. My mother loved to entertain. She would bake and prepare the house. I loved to bake with her, and Christmas baking was my favorite. She kept all the Swedish traditions. We made Swedish meatballs, breads, and cookies. Swedish cookies had lots of spices, which filled the house with smells like cardamom, ginger, nutmeg, and almonds. Sometimes, we made the dough one day and cooked the cookies or bread the next day. Mom was happy in the kitchen and so was I. She was loving and patient with me while we were cooking. She made special sandwiches for our company and always allowed me to help. Some of my favorite sandwiches were on small pumpernickel bread slices topped with cucumbers.

Dressing up and clothes were never important to me. I didn't really care. We had to dress up for Easter, and that was the only time I remember looking forward to getting into pretty clothes. Mom made all our school clothes. Every summer, we got to pick out the patterns and the material for our new school clothes, and she would sew them for all of us. When I was in seventh grade, she made this pretty dress with pastel stripes. I do remember liking that particular dress.

Basically, I was a tomboy at heart. I preferred to be outside running and playing rather than being inside. I was forever asking, "Please, can I go out now?" Once I was outside, I felt the freedom it gave me. My favorite activities were hiking, walking through the woods, climbing the wall at the church, or going behind the grocery store and climbing up on top of the shed's roof. A neighbor boy and I would sometimes go to the lake, catch crawfish with our hands, and put them in old coffee cans for hours and hours. That was my idea of fun and freedom.

Every day after school during my elementary years was another day to create a new game. We often collected berries, weeds, and sticks and put them in a pot to make a pretend stew. If the outside fireplace was burning our trash that day, we could heat up our stew.

I could handle the rest of life if I could get outside every day and enjoy the great outdoors, that is until that day came: October 31, 1967. Then my world changed forever!

The Accident

The driver was speeding down our street, going 55 mph in a 35 mph zone on Halloween day, 1967.

I had been begging all afternoon, "Mom, please let me go across the street and get Kathy."

I was jumping up and down. This was exciting stuff! I was eleven years old, and Kathy and I were dressed up like twin little girls. We were both in pink dresses, our long hair up in pigtails with pink ribbons, and carrying big lollipops to suck on. The year

19

before, we were twin babies with bottles. Kathy was my very best friend.

"Mom, please, oh please, can I go get Kathy now?" I asked again for the hundredth time.

"Yes, Karen, you can go get Kathy. You be really careful crossing the street, though," Mom said.

Finally, I was free to go! That was the last thing I remember on that Halloween day. I woke up three days later in the local hospital.

Suddenly, the lights were too bright and blinding. I couldn't keep my eyes open. I couldn't focus. I didn't hear anything. I tried, but I couldn't move.

As I started to come out of it, I felt like I was in a cozy, comforting dream. It was like I was horizontal, warm all over, and floating on clouds. The clouds were gray, soft, cottony, and fluffy. There were no other colors, but it was so peaceful. I wanted to stay in that place. I felt so warm and safe. I never wanted to leave, but God had other plans.

Why won't anything move?

When I was finally able to focus, the bright lights on the ceiling hurt my eyes. *Where was I and where had I been?* I was hungry, but I could not seem to talk. As I gradually came out of the fog, I realized I had tubes coming out of every conceivable location in my body. *Why can't I talk?* I thought. My eyes searched for something familiar, screaming the panic that was rising up within me.

I felt rather than saw my mother's hand on me and heard her say, "She's awake!"

Suddenly, there was activity everywhere. When things calmed down a little, a nurse bent over me and slowly explained I had been in a coma for three days after being hit by that speeding car on Halloween.

As I tried to speak, I could not take a breath. I was breathing through a tube in my neck. In order to speak, I would have had to close a hole in the tube to get any sound to come out of my mouth. That was impossible at the moment, though. Realizing I was trying to communicate, they handed me a piece of paper. I tried to write, though I couldn't get my hand and arm to work right. My brain was telling me I was hungry. I wanted a hamburger, but I could only spell out the word "HAM." One of the nurses asked if I was hungry and wanted a hamburger. Relieved she understood me, I blinked. I heard an uproar in the room. I think they were happy about something, but I was so confused!

One thought I had as I tried to make sense out of what had happened to me was that I would not be afraid to die. The place that I had been for the last few days was so comforting and warm. Even though there were no colors, I had a sense of warmth, and comfort; it was like I was waiting in the womb for a rebirth.

The next few months in the hospital were a blur. I slowly got disconnected from feeding tubes, tubes to go to the bathroom, and a tube that went into my left lung. According to the doctors, a broken rib had punctured that lung. My whole left side was paralyzed, but slowly, day after day, with physical therapy, I regained strength—all except in my left hand. My total time of healing was probably over a year.

Learning to walk was definitely the most challenging experience. My right leg had been completely broken at the tibia, and plates were put in to hold the leg together. I could no longer lift up the toes on my right foot, so I walked with a limp. With a paralyzed left side, and a damaged right leg, the team of doctors gave me a leg brace so I could walk.

I threw the brace across the room, and stated vehemently, "It will be a cold day in hell before I wear that in public!"

This is the moment my "survivor self" took over.

Each and every day had its new challenges during the next few years. I returned to the seventh grade, but I do not remember much about that year. I think that I either blocked out the accident from my memory or the traumatic brain injury blurred my memories.

Wisdom Nuggets

We all have childhood memories and experiences that influence our life as adults.

List some of your fondest childhood memories.

List some of the things that you did not enjoy about your childhood.

Relationships with our parents and siblings also have a major impact on our adult lives.

Detail your relationships with you mother, father, and siblings.

Were there any other significant people in your life who impacted your life?

Questions to Ponder and Journal About

One thought that I had after waking up from the coma was I will never be afraid to die.

What does life after death mean to you?

Do you believe in God?

Read these scripture verses and begin to open your heart and mind to God. It is only through a relationship with Him that you can truly identify and deal with those "emotional monsters" from your childhood that have kept you in bondage.

Isaiah 40:29 says, "He gives strength to the weary and increases the power of the weak."

Who is giving you this strength?

God has said, "Never will I leave you; never will I forsake you" (Hebrews 13:5 NIV).

What does this verse mean to you personally?

I am so proud of you! You have just begun a journey that will move you on the road to recovery. Don't worry; you are never alone!

Pray: *God, create in me a clean heart so that I may be of service to You.*

CHAPTER 2

DEVELOPING YEARS

*Beloved, let us love one another, for love is from God;
and everyone who loves is born of God and knows God.*
(1 John 4:7)

Challenging Years After the Accident

L ate that spring, I remember when I was called down to the nurse's office at school for a routine spinal check.

"Please stand up straight," said the school nurse.

I thought, *I am standing up straight! Can't she see that!* I was angry, trying my best to stand up without a bend in my back. That day my parents received a call from the school indicating I needed to be seen by an orthopedic doctor for spinal surgery. It was less than one year after my accident.

That next fall, I was taken to Boston Children's Hospital for back surgery, which required a tortuous process of re-forming my back with what seemed a medieval procedure. My curvature of the spine was called kyphosis, which meant I had a really big hunched back. I was put in a cast from my neck to my knees, and then they made a split in the cast from one side of my waist to the other. This split was made wider and wider every day until my back had been reshaped and I was contorted into a backbend.

Once they were happy with the shape of the spine, they took part of my left leg bone and fused my back together.

As the danger for infection lessened, they sent me home, and there I remained in that cast for six months.

One of the biggest frustrations I had as a young teenager was that I could do nothing on my own. This included reaching my private parts! I was dependent on my mother for everything. All I could do was lie in bed with the cast on my entire body. This was my life, my mother's life, and my little sister's life for six months, caring for me. My dad worked three jobs to help pay the expenses.

I was able to attend eighth grade in my bedroom through an intercom system that allowed me to hear the class and answer questions by buzzing in to them. My best friend, Kathy, carried the box from class to class so that I could pass that grade. In some sense, I think she felt guilty about my accident because I'd been hit by the car crossing the street to her house that day in October.

Once the body cast was off, I was put into a walking cast for six months and a body brace for six months after that. That about explains my life as a "middle-schooler."

Today, I teach in a middle school with special needs students!

Surviving became a way of life that I became used to, and I must say, I was very proficient at it. I was known for my strength and perseverance. I never looked at life's challenges as drudgery, as so many did, but enjoyed conquering each and every new challenge. Also burning within me, a new desire to know and understand God emerged. I felt that He wanted me here on this earth for a reason, and I wanted to know why.

You might be wondering whether my grandmother had any influence on the spiritual answers in my life. I would have to say, in her own peculiar way, she showed me there was more to life than eyes could see.

During the next few years, I went church-hopping, religion-hopping, and even dabbled in the Tarot cards. My grandmother was into astrology and those cards. She had even predicted that something terrible was going to happen the day of my accident—she thought *she* was going to die!

I graduated from high school, but not until I'd spent my senior year in an alternative school called Dynamy. I applied and was accepted to this alternative school because even my parents knew that after all those experiences, my life's path was taking an alternative route. It was the best year I had in high school. We climbed the White Mountains and worked in internships, all challenges that I could succeed in.

After I graduated, I went off to college to study psychology and elementary education. During my senior year in college, I applied to go on a student exchange trip to the Canary Islands to do my student teaching. Living with the natives there, I was invited to go to a church service, and I gave my life to the Lord in 1978. I found that traveling to foreign countries gave me a sense of freedom to live and choose the way I was meant to live.

Once I returned to the States, I searched for a church and found a Pentecostal church that fed my soul. It was there, in Worcester, Massachusetts, that I developed a strong relationship with my Lord and Savior.

With a paralyzed left hand, playing piano and violin were not possible, but I wanted music in my life. I could sing, I thought, except I had no natural talent. That did not stop the survivor in me. *Practice, practice, and practice until you get it*, I told myself. I cleaned the house of my vocal teacher in exchange for voice lessons.

That was the beginning of my vocal career. It was my hobby, and I loved it. I sang in a Pentecostal choir of sixty members, the Worcester Symphony choir of over two hundred members, small church choirs, gospel groups, and more. I even sang at weddings. I now had music back in my life.

At the age of twenty-two, I had no desire to get married or have kids. I wanted to see the world! I had graduated from college with a degree in psychology and a degree in education. I could teach anywhere, so I started applying overseas. My first position was in San Juan, Puerto Rico, where I taught third grade. A year after that, I accepted a position in Ecuador, and a year after that, in Taiwan.

During the time period from Ecuador to Taiwan, I fell in love with a Christian man who taught me not only how to fall more in love with God, but also how to love myself. He really taught me how to love myself through reading the Bible. You might say, "Isn't that being selfish, to love yourself?" No, it is in loving who you are so that you can love others unconditionally and not love them through eyes that are clouded with needs.

Ecuador

I got a job teaching third grade at an American school in Guayaquil, Ecuador. I had no prior knowledge of the country or the culture, but had learned Spanish in Puerto Rico (although Puerto Rican Spanish is a language of its own).

As I walked down the runway out of the plane, my first image of Ecuador was a military man with a machine gun. I really didn't know who I was at that time in my life, but I had no fear; everything was an adventure. I just loved life and everything it brought my way.

At first, I stayed in a rundown hotel in downtown Guayaquil, and later found out how very lucky I was not to have been robbed. During my first few days there, I walked around town as if I owned the country, and believe it or not, nothing happened to me. Surely the hand of the Lord protected me at that time. My checkpoint person picked me up two days later and brought me to a really nice house. She said that I would be living in this house that belong to missionaries who were on furlough. They liked to have people living in the house for safety's sake.

My new house was on Calle Prima, First Street, and it came with a maid. Her name was, Rosita. She was around fifteen and lived at the house. This house provided her shelter because her family could not. In exchange for shelter, she was my maid. That took a while to get used to. I wanted to take care of her, but to do so was insulting to her. She cooked, cleaned, did laundry, and even made my coffee in the morning.

Once settled in my new house and new job, I was invited to the home of the second grade teacher and the principal for a Bible study. They told me that they had been trying to get a local Chinese Christian man who lived near me to come to the Bible study. He had a truck, which could provide me with transportation to their out-of-the-way home in Guayaquil. I called this man week after week, but he had no interest in going. With no luck on the phone, I finally decided to visit him in person, hoping beyond hope to change his mind. I wanted to go to the Bible study and needed transportation.

Wearing heavy wooden clogs, one could hear me coming from across the country. He told me later that when he heard my shoes, he knew that his life was about to be transformed. That was the beginning of our relationship. Felipe, or should I say, Lin Fa Pin, invited me into his home. At the door, I was expected to remove my shoes. His home had the décor of a Chinese home. The walls were covered with decorative fans and Chinese writings. He invited me for Chinese tea. We talked and he told me that he had terrible night vision and could not drive at night. The Bible studies were at night, so he would not be able to go. I told him that I could drive a standard-shift truck and that we *could* go. We went the very next week.

Week after week, Felipe and I got to know each other and became each other's confidants. Felipe was probably thirty years older than I, but I really could not tell you his exact age. He practiced Tai Chi every day, and was in much better shape than I. I was about fifty pounds overweight at that time in my life. Felipe would come to visit me and we would spend afternoons studying the Bible. We would share verses with each other every day.

Then it happened. One day, I was emotional about something and Felipe kissed my tears. I looked up at him and saw in his eyes that it was more than a loving kiss from a father figure. Then he kissed me. That was the beginning of a beautiful, wonderful, growing year in my life. Yet it was not that simple. Felipe was only separated from his wife. They had been separated for sixteen years.

As the year went on in Ecuador, I taught, studied the Bible, and lost fifty pounds. I learned to love the Lord, to love myself, and to love Felipe. One day he got word that his wife was dying. I prayed and was told by the Lord that he needed to go back to his wife. He prayed and received the same message.

Felipe called me, Kyloon, which represented my first and last names in Chinese, and he stressed how much he loved me. Because he loved me, he wanted me to go back to the States and have children, two girls. His prophecy came true. We parted loving each other, but were never to see each other again.

Home again at the age of twenty-nine, my biological clock started to kick in. Now I wanted kids and I wanted to settle down. As I settled back into life in the United States, I turned my attention to finding a husband and beginning the next season of my life.

"An assertive communicator's belief of communication is you matter and so do I."

— Danny Silk,
Keep Your Love On: Connection, Communication & Boundaries

Wisdom Nuggets

"When we don't set boundaries around our relationships, we attract disrespectful relationships into our lives. We must protect what's important to us, and what's important to us are the things we say 'yes' to. Healthy relationships truly are the most vulnerable, meaningful and satisfying of human experiences. The foundation of a healthy relationship is unconditional love and acceptance." -Danny Silk, *Keep Your Love On: Connection, Communication & Boundaries*

I turned my attentions to finding a husband and beginning the next season of my life. However, I tried to do this on my own and did not seek God's guidance and paid the price. God's instructions about marital relationships are clear to us.

Do not be bound together with unbelievers; for what partnership have righteousness and lawlessness, or what fellowship has light with darkness?
(2 Corinthians 6:14)

If you are looking for a spouse, take the time to stop and ask yourself:
Am I so lonely and afraid that I cannot wait for the right man/woman to come along?

Why should I wait for the right mate?

Why it is so important for me to bring my petitions to God?

Have I made a list of my perfect mate's qualities and prayed over it day and night?

Questions to Ponder and Journal About

Growing into adolescence, what traumas do you remember?

What hidden pains, wounds, or events might you have buried during this time frame before you decided to marry?

If you are married, did you go before God asking for your right soul mate?

Did you write your perfect mate list and bring it to God?

Write details about meeting your spouse or significant other.

Were there any other events during your growing and young adult years that you have buried and would prefer to leave buried? Why?

Have you learned to love yourself through the eyes of God? Explain.

Did you set boundaries around yourself to display yourself as valuable and precious while dating?

Remember, this journal is only for you and God. The purpose of this book is for you to ultimately stand naked before God, leaving no stone unturned. As you learn to expose the negative wounds, hurts, and pains that you so neatly buried in your heart, the devil will lose his grip on your negative thoughts. You will learn to let go and let God fill you with His unending love.

Pray: *Create in me a clean heart so that I may be of service to You.*

CHAPTER 3

KYLOON AND HER "MONSTER"

Dear friend, do not imitate what is evil but what is good.
Anyone who does what is good is from God.
Anyone who does what is evil has not seen God.
(3 John 1:11 NIV)

Once back in the United States, Kyloon, now in her late twenties, felt her biological clock ticking. She knew that she needed to find to a man to marry if she was ever going to have a family. Through various friends and family, she finally met a man who was, she thought, a good catch. This handsome man, who happened to work in the education field, came from a good family and was, most importantly, her age.

As she contemplated spending her life with this man who had asked her to marry, Kyloon asked herself, *Why does this man seem so unhappy inside?*

Questions, doubts, and fears began to emerge within her heart, though she tried to ignore them. This is where the "monster" loves to live and devour.

Kyloon dated this man off and on for two years. As time went on, she was outwardly content, but her spirit felt differently. He asked her to marry him many times, but she would not give in because of the nagging feeling that something was off. The ability to resist his proposals lasted until she finally saw another portion of her dream come true. Though she had wondered if it was even possible, she discovered that she was pregnant. *A baby, my dream*, she thought. A baby at her age prompted her to give in, and she said yes to marriage. She felt she was ready to face this new season of her life.

Whatever you have learned or received or heard from me, or seen in me—put it into practice. And the God of peace will be with you.
(Philippians 4:9)

Hiding from the Monster

A fool finds pleasure in wicked schemes,
but a person of understanding delights in wisdom.
(Proverbs 10:23)

The monster that she was about to face was not an individual, but a series of events that would lead to negative spiritual entrapments and ultimately change her way of viewing the world. Kyloon had her life set before her to raise her family and be the wife and mother that she always knew she could be. Her pregnancy and expectancy toward motherhood was everything she thought it would be. She felt great and everything was going her way. She even decided to add a certificate in teaching to make her more employable.

There was only one exception to her happiness. Her husband periodically raged at her for no apparent reason. His rages and anger were verbal darts directed at her, even if he had been angry at the light bulb. Kyloon wanted to do right by her husband, but when he told her it was her fault in the way she interpreted the situation, she couldn't understand how she had gotten it so wrong. Hiding from his anger and her own feelings of confusion became a natural state for Kyloon. However, what was really going on inside was she was losing her own identity.

Kyloon stopped *feeling* the verbal darts that were meant to hurt her as a form of self-defense. Little did Kyloon know, this also meant she was stopping the feelings of joy, love, and peace, too.

She found motherhood to be all that she had hoped it would be. She loved being a mother, but soon the wife part became a challenge. She wanted so much to have peace in her house. Kyloon joined a local church group, helped the poor, and sang in a choir. She had a best friend who was part of this same group. This friend also had a boy the same age as her daughter. The next ten years were spent hiding from the "anger monster" to create the peace and harmony that she so wanted for herself and her now two daughters. At least this is what she thought.

> "If your heart is governed by fear, then much of what you communicate is actually designed to hide what really is going on inside."
> —Danny Silk,
> *Keep Your Love On: Connection, Communication & Boundaries*

One can only hide for so long before the monster will catch up with you. In the most unexpected places, the monster will reappear. Chopping down a Christmas tree, going on a cruise, and driving to a summer cottage on the lake can turn into emotional battles. Her defense was to continue to hide from the monster and the feelings that went with it. Kyloon finally resigned herself to this dilemma. She knew that there was no taming the monster within someone else.

That's when she decided to try counseling, desperately trying to understand the monsters within her own being, which she instinctively knew were growing and taking residence in her innermost self. Their names were **Fear** and **Guilt.** Guilt results from beginning to identify with the verbal darts and calling them truths, Kyloon had begun to lose herself to the lies.

If she had known some of the basic truths about how to be an assertive communicator and not a passive one, she could have responded, "We can talk later when you choose to be responsible and tell me what's really going on." Instead, Kyloon became passive, internalized the situation, and blamed herself for the disconnection in their relationship.

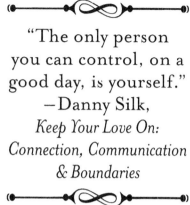

"The only person you can control, on a good day, is yourself."
—Danny Silk,
Keep Your Love On:
Connection, Communication
& Boundaries

And the peace of God, which transcends all understanding,
will guard your hearts and your minds in Christ Jesus.
(Philippians 4:7)

Facing the Monster

Turn from evil and do good; seek peace and pursue it.
(Psalm 34:14)

One night when Kyloon was alone, she started writing in her journal as the counselor had suggested, hoping it might help her better understand what had just happened. Perhaps, it would explain how and why she came to face the monster:

My journey to recovery. My move to the new state in New England where my husband got his job was not as easy as expected. I was able to get my house unpacked and get ready for school, but with no days to enjoy the summer. I still have books to put away and walls to paint, but these things can happen whenever I can get a spare moment.

My wake-up call that something was wrong was when I contemplated suicide as an alternative to living here with my husband. What has happened to me, the fun-loving child? Instead of looking at myself as I should have, I decided to get help for my husband and his anger, rages, and all-around inability to cope. Helping him with his anger didn't work, so I was left staring at myself in the mirror.

At first, my husband agreed to go to counseling, so we went together. After a few near-tear experiences, as my husband [could] really be dramatic with the counselor, the counselor began to sympathize with him. She explained clearly and emphatically that his reactions to situations were just a result of his type of personality. I could not believe [it]. I snapped inside. She, the counselor, had no idea of the personal abuse that I'd been through living with a man who acted out his emotions though anger, especially with his tongue. Well, I knew at that moment that I couldn't get all my help from her, but I had to also get it elsewhere.

Where did I go? I went to God. That night during my prayer time, alone time with God, I stood naked before God as He told me to strip down all my emotions before Him and let them go, each and every one.

Finally, brothers and sisters, whatever is true, whatever is noble, whatever is right, whatever is pure, whatever is lovely, whatever is admirable — if anything is excellent or praiseworthy — think about such things.
(Philippians 4:8)

Arguing with God

Do all things without grumbling or arguing. (Philippians 2:14)

I'm not sure I can do this, Kyloon thought, *I have been hiding for so long.* It was either that, or she would have to live with the reality that suicide might be the only option, given the emotions that were inside her. Then she remembered: *I'm not a coward—* and, therefore, she decided to open up to God and start to *feel.* "Create in me a clean heart, oh Lord, so that I may be of service to You" became her routine prayer every morning.

Her emotions were exposed and she began to release what was trapped within her. It was not pretty. She cried for two days.

She felt raw, as though her heart was an open wound and like she was wearing her emotions on her sleeve. Even a Christmas song could make her cry for no apparent reason.

Her emotions had many layers. The first one she experienced was **anger**. This lasted two to three days. This anger was aimed at no one in particular, but more at the situation. To Kyloon, anger was at the root of "all evil."

The second emotion was profound sadness. It was more like grief. It came from her belly. It was during this time that her sister called and told her that their mother was failing. Kyloon had just seen her mother at Thanksgiving and knew how sick she was, but did not want to acknowledge it. She spent a day mourning the loss she knew was in the near future.

Next came **fear**. This emotion was sneaky. It came in her dreams. For the next four nights, she had nightmares. Men were trying to kill her, and the only way to escape was to wake up. Her heart would be racing and pounding with the fear that there was no escape.

Do I fear my husband that much? she asked herself. *I fear his anger, not him personally. There is no escape from it.*

This is a classical relational dynamic created by powerless people, like Kyloon and her husband. It is called triangulation. When you believe that other people are scary and unsafe, you still need to get your needs met. Therefore, in your relationship you can play victim, rescuer or bad guy. Kyloon played the role of the rescuer who wanted to save and fix her husband by making him happy.

Family events and holidays often triggered her husband's emotional outbreaks. The week before Christmas, the whole family had decided to spend a day celebrating the holiday with other people from their town. They traveled around from noon to six p.m., going to various locations in town. They sang songs at a bonfire and had food and drinks at a local gathering place. Normally, Kyloon's husband would not have been able to do it, but he was trying. She and her oldest daughter kept looking over at him, waiting for an outburst or a cue that they would have to leave. Her daughter had even questioned Kyloon earlier about her father going since he always ruined things when he got angry. But this day, he really appeared to be trying. Well, actually he showed no emotion, sat off by himself and did not talk to anyone. This allowed Kyloon and her daughters to have a good time.

The next night was the first night that Kyloon was able to sleep without nightmares. She kept herself up until midnight, hoping exhaustion would help. It did. *Perhaps she was done with that emotion,* she thought. *What next, God?*

Kyloon decided she did not want to hide those emotions any longer, especially since it seemed to be helping her husband. She went back to the same counselor and shared those layers of emotions and frustration with her.

I can do all this through him who gives me strength.
(Philippians 4:13)

Running from the Monster

Therefore, my beloved, flee from idolatry. (1 Corinthians 10:14)

But when I am afraid, I will put my trust in you. I praise God for what he has promised. I trust in God, so why should I be afraid? What can mere mortals do to me? (Psalm 56:3–4 NLT)

Kyloon was seeing a change in her husband, a desire to stop his anger. At least, she wanted to think and believe that. He tried to spend more time with the two girls and avoid getting angry with Kyloon.

Then one afternoon, the atmosphere became heavy in the house. Kyloon's husband was in the formal living room, separated from the family, lying on the couch in one of his depressions. There was nothing she could do. Trying only made things worse. During these times, separation and quiet were the best mode of treatment for his state of mind. As a matter of fact, for the past ten years of marriage, he had always had a separate space to retreat to in each of their three houses.

Then the unthinkable happened. While she was doing her normal chores of trying to bring normalcy to her family, her husband emerged from the living room glowing. Perhaps *glowing* cannot accurately describe how he looked. His eyes, his face, everything looked different.

He then stated in an almost stunned voice, "I just had an encounter with God. I got down on my knees and prayed to God and told Him that I just couldn't take this agony anymore. He then filled me with His Spirit!"

He was actually smiling. That was the beginning of the most beautiful six months of their marriage. Kyloon's husband began attending church services and going to other believers' homes with her and the kids. No one could believe his transformation. They were all amazed at how happy he was. Kyloon's husband was saved, renewed, restored, and happy. She was so happy—for both of them.

However, this happiness and transformational state lasted a very short span in the marriage. Soon the anger monster began to reappear. Church attendance declined and eventually stopped. The anger monster began to take over his life once again, but this time with even more force. Kyloon and her husband never learned how to communicate and make a connection based on unconditional love. They never developed a trust cycle where each could communicate their own needs and have their needs satisfied by the other. This stood in the way of their healing.

Three years later, Kyloon asked her husband for a separation. She could no longer keep forgiving him for his angry episodes, clean up after him, and protect the family at the same time. Her husband left for six months and attended marriage counseling. Kyloon also attended both individual and couple's marriage counseling. It was during this time that she began to understand the power of **fear**. After a year of counseling, she felt stronger and made a promise to herself that she would not allow the same cycle to reoccur with her and her husband ever again.

However, when they moved back in together, the marriage counseling stopped. Within a year, the anger monster began to weasel its way back into the relationship. Old behaviors returned. By the time they planned to move to Maine, the old behaviors had established themselves in all their sneaky and perverted ways. However, the two of them were so busy trying to buy and sell houses for the move, the monster was able to sneak in without being noticed.

Within a few months of the move, Kyloon knew that, once again, she had been "caught by the monster." This time she tried to make the identity of the monster known to her husband. Once again, he made sure that Kyloon knew that *she* was the one who had the problems, not him.

To Kyloon's surprise, the new job and the atmosphere of their new home proved to be quite good. She was having great success in her job, with two major administrative observations behind her. She felt at home here. She fit.

Kyloon found that the people of the state had the personalities of the hippies who had moved there to find peace, love, and joy. It reminded her of the seventies, when one could wear hiking boots with skirts and enjoy long hair and lots of music. She felt right at home. People genuinely cared for one another. People laughed and smiled. She felt the love in the community, and felt that this was a place where she could live in harmony with herself and others.

The greatest advantage for Kyloon was that she could begin to establish her own self-esteem. If measured on a scale of one to ten, when she moved there her self-esteem level was in the negative range. With her increase of positive self-esteem, Kyloon began to feel she could stand up for herself in the future. Kyloon wanted more than anything to move from a powerless position to a powerful position, but still did not have the skill set to do so.

With failed jobs, an unstable marriage, and dealing with her own disabilities, Kyloon's self-worth had totaled up to not much more than their house pet. In fact, Kyloon knew that their dog received more unconditional love and attention than she did from her husband. It was going to be an uphill battle to overcome the past, but the survivor within her began to plant the seeds of hope. However, she still did not have the power or skills to really face the monsters head on.

Creating a Generational Influence

Since neither one of them trusted or communicated with the other, their needs could not be met. Running from the monster became a way of life for Kyloon. She couldn't hide any longer because she now knew the truth of its existence. Running seemed the best way. She continued this approach until she saw the damage it was causing to her daughters, especially the older one.

Her older daughter had a boyfriend who was sweet, kind, loving, but who was not ready to settle into the long-term relationship or commitment the girl craved. As a result, he periodically did as he wanted and saw other girls. Kyloon's daughter would cry, be hurt, but could not let him go.

One day Kyloon saw herself in her daughter when she said to Kyloon, "I'm too weak to let him go, even if I know I should. I love him and need him."

Another example of the damage occurred during a trip with Kyloon and her two daughters. Her husband had given her a key to her daughter's car. She and her younger daughter were to pick up her older daughter with that car at the bus station two hours away. On their return home, they decided that a stop at Dunkin' Donuts was a must. Kyloon locked the car, took the keys, and they went inside. Upon returning to the car, the key her husband had given her would not unlock the doors. Panic began to rise in Kyloon, but she immediately put on a smiling face and said that it was not a problem; she would simply call Dad to bring the original set of keys.

One would think that this would be a simple call, but the family knew better. After the call was made, the feeling of **fear** began to emerge. What surprised Kyloon was the extent to which the fear was embedded in her oldest daughter. As the time grew near for her dad's arrival with the keys, that **fear** grew. The girl increasingly felt that her dad would blame her for the failing lock, even though he was the one who had given the bad key to her mom. She felt **guilty** because it was her car. Her daughter paced by the restaurant door and eventually went outside to wait for him. She didn't want her **guilt** and **fear** to be seen by others.

Sadly, Kyloon realized that she could not protect her daughter from the fear monster and the lies of the devil. Kyloon's passive communication practice was passed on to her daughter. Neither one of them knew how to set boundaries, so they decided to remain passive to maintain peace in their relationships.

Kyloon's younger daughter never had much of a bond with her father. Luckily, she did not internalize the anger as her older sister did, but instead externalized her frustration. She has been verbal since the day she was born; therefore, her father and she never understood each other. He internalize everything, just like his first daughter. Their second daughter was a survivor, like her mom. She would rather see the glass half full, but unlike her mom, she made sure someone else filled it for her. Most of the time, she tried to dominate her mother. She, too, needed some sort of control in this family.

Preparing for Christmas vacation was a full-time job in their household. The week before Christmas was spent in school, so time was scarce. There was a full day of school on Friday, and on Saturday morning the family took off for a Christmas party at Kyloon's sister's house. After the party there, the family was headed to Vermont for another family gathering. Bags were packed, presents were wrapped, and food prepared and placed in bags in the trunk. They were ready by 8:30 a.m.

Christmastime had always been difficult for Kyloon's husband. Many people who suffer from depression and anxiety find the holidays difficult. He was no different. By the time they got to his sister's house located on a sixty-acre horse farm with six horses, he was irritated. The dirt road was muddy due to the unseasonably warm weather they'd been having. As he drove up the road, the car slipped and slid in the mud, causing the car to swerve. By the time they arrived at the house, the anger monster made itself present as their companion. Instead of arriving with the love and joy of the Christmas holiday, Kyloon's family arrived carrying the weight of the anger monster.

The week after Christmas, Kyloon's oldest daughter went to Boston to visit her boyfriend's home. Kyloon, her husband, and their younger daughter were together at home for the next five days. There were many projects around the house that needed to be completed. Kyloon wanted to build a cabinet in the bathroom, install a new light fixture, and paint the walls. Her husband was going to build a shed in the backyard with the help of a fellow teacher.

It was during this time that Kyloon stopped running from the monster and started observing the monster for what it truly was.

Do not be anxious about anything, but in every situation, by
prayer and petition, with thanksgiving,
present your requests to God.
(Philippians 4:6)

Observing the Monster

When I applied my mind to know wisdom and to observe the
labor that is done on earth—people getting no sleep day or night.
(Ecclesiastes 8:16)

What this means is that we cannot know and understand everything. It is beyond our comprehension. This is where faith steps in. Kyloon had a lengthy conversation with her friend about her husband. This friend truly understood the depth of his anger and the existing dynamics of their relationship.

After expressing her fears about the bathroom project and the anger it would create in her husband, her friend's reply was, "He will be angry no matter what you do."

Right then and there, the light went on in Kyloon's head. *She's right,* thought Kyloon. So when they returned home, Kyloon decided to watch her husband from an outside perspective. It was almost like an out-of-body experience. She could no longer feel his anger. She had removed herself from his emotional bondage by not allowing herself to feel it. She was an outsider observing the monster.

The next five days for Kyloon were like watching a movie. She did not attend to her husband's anger or react to it, but was just able to simply observe. Without a sounding board for his anger, he blamed whoever and whatever came near him.

During this time, Kyloon proceeded to start work on the bathroom, which meant tearing down the existing light fixture first. Meanwhile, her husband was outside working with his friend on the shed, which had come in a kit.

One would think that this situation would not be alarming, but to her husband it was. First the instructions were misplaced. Instead of taking ownership for misplacing them, he blamed the company for not sending them. They faxed him another set. Then he thought there were missing parts, and again he blamed the company. However, Kyloon helped him locate those in the box under some papers. Later, when Kyloon asked for assistance with some electrical problem on her project, he got upset that she was working on the bathroom at all. This was something they had discussed at length, and they had bought the parts together.

He does not hear me when I speak, or value my opinions, Kyloon thought.

Another sign that things were not well with him occurred when he refused to eat anything that was served to him and his friend that day. This made it awkward for his friend to eat anything while he was there helping.

The next day continued in the same manner. He refused to eat breakfast. In midmorning, he ran into the house from the shed holding his arm and complaining of cramps. While he screamed in pain, Kyloon tried to help, telling him to put the arm under hot water. Without proper nutrition and hydration, one's body will naturally rebel against constant hammering and cold weather. It was just another reason for the anger monster to take over.

Five days observing the anger monster from the outside made Kyloon realize that she didn't want to live under its clutches anymore. *Now what?* she wondered. She felt she had to talk to him about what she had observed and the impact that it had on her, but she was afraid. She knew if she tried to talk to him, he would only become angrier. The anger monster was relentless.

The anticipation and anxiety of wanting to talk to her husband made the living situation almost intolerable. As she walked upstairs to talk to him, her hands were clenched and her body was shaking. She had to share the truth with him. She also wanted to show her daughters that it was okay to stand up for oneself. As she spoke to her husband of her observations, the retaliation began.

"You are the one with relationship problems and personality problems," he said loudly, shaking his head. "It started in the past. You have never been successful with relationships. Who are you to talk?"

After this attempt to communicate with her husband, Kyloon went back downstairs and laid down on the couch.

About fifteen minutes later, her oldest daughter asked, "What's up?"

Kyloon told her that she had talked to her dad about his behavior that day and that he was angry with everyone. This anger was difficult to live with, to say the least.

Kyloon's daughter said, "I'm proud of you, Mom!"

Kyloon then told her, with tears in her eyes, that Dad had verbally attacked her.

"Did you expect anything less?" her daughter said matter-of-factly.

Shortly thereafter, Kyloon and her husband separated. Looking back, Kyloon realized if she had been an assertive communicator, she might have approached that conversation differently. Her first goal would have been to understand her husband's feelings about the day. Next, she would have stated her feelings about the situation, and how it affected her and the children. Lastly, she would have stated her love, and ask if she could be of assistance in anyway without judgement.

> He said to them,
> "You are the ones who justify yourselves in the eyes of others,
> but God knows your hearts.
> What people value highly is detestable in God's sight."
> (Luke 15:16)

Wisdom Nuggets

There are five categories of behavior we use to communicate messages of love. One person may view love differently and have different love needs. In order to move towards an individual with love messages, you have to understand which love message they require to feel loved.

Take a moment and read these brief descriptions. Identify your method of communicating and receiving love. Then identify the way your spouse and each of your children convey love.

1. Touch – physical contact
2. Acts of Service – intentional acts of kindness
3. Gifts – physical tokens of love
4. Quality Time – when you want to spend time with your partner to feel love
5. Words of Affirmation – words and body language of love and spiritual connection

We want to conceive our reality as good or perfect so we are unwilling to spend the time to deal with the past that binds wounds, pains, failures, insecurities, abandonment, etc., in our hearts. It is so much easier to pretend that they just don't exist. **Guess what?** They will fester into open wounds and cause you or your loved ones *more* pain than when the original pain manifested. This is true selfishness when you do not deal with old pain.

Perhaps you like to stay in the pain because it is comfortable and comforting in some way. *Does this describe you?*

Perhaps you do not know how to live without the pain. *Does this describe you?*

Is there another reason you have observed in your life why you have not been able to deal with your old pain?

Do not fret, because we never have to do this alone. Once we have accepted the truth that our Savior, Jesus died for us, He becomes our all in all.

Read these scriptures and begin to realize how much He desires to become your protector, your shield, and your strength.

Psalm 32:7 says God is my _____

Psalm 28:7 says the Lord is my _____

Psalm 46:1 says God is my _____

Questions to Ponder and Journal About

Make a list of all the things that you are afraid of.

Make a list of all the things that you don't want to deal with in your life—all those that were easier left untouched than dealt with. List each and every one.

What do you feel guilty about?

What events/people in your life caused you the most pain?

Which kind of communicator are you?
a. Passive (reluctant to enter in and volunteer information)
b. Aggressive (pushing your opinions on others)
c. Passive/Aggressive (appearing to be passive but only to get back at the other person later)
d. Assertive (standing firm on what's true while being loving and kind)

Which method of conveying did you discover you require?

Which method did you discover your relational partner requires?

How is this information going to help you improve your relationship?

And He has said to me,
"My grace is sufficient for you, for power is perfected in weakness."
Most gladly, therefore, I will rather boast about my weaknesses,
so that the power of Christ may dwell in me.
Therefore I am well content with weaknesses, with insults,
with distresses, with persecutions, with difficulties, for Christ's
sake; for when I am weak, then I am strong.
(2 Corinthians 12:9-10)

When we give everything to our God in our weakness, He can work in us. If we think we are strong, our egos get in the way. God cannot work with a hardened heart. When we are weak, we are vulnerable. Each and every time we allow God to work in our lives by stepping back, we allow His divine power to come into our lives and transform us. The true deciding factor in our healing is our decision to humble ourselves, accept our weaknesses, and allow God to be made strong in us. We are His heirs, and He wants nothing more than to give us our inheritance of righteousness. He cannot do that when we are full of stubbornness, shame, guilt, fear, and the like. He is waiting for us to let each and every thing that is binding us on our list to be handed over to Him to release us from the shackles of the past.

Let us break their chains and throw off their shackles.
(Psalm 2:3)

One of the things David modeled for us is don't hold it in. In Psalm 39:1–4, David explains what happened when he tried to keep his struggles a secret:

I said..."I will not say anything while evil people are near." I kept quiet, not saying a word...But my suffering only grew worse, and I was overcome with anxiety. The more I thought, the more troubled I became; I could not keep from asking: "Lord, how long will I live? When will I die? Tell me how soon my life will end." (GNT)

Pray: *Create in me a clean heart so that I may be of service to You.*

CHAPTER 4

FINDING HELP

Now the Lord is that Spirit:
and where the Spirit of the Lord [is], there [is] liberty.
But we all, with open face beholding as in a glass the glory of the
Lord, are changed into the same image from glory to glory,
[even] as by the Spirit of the Lord.
(2 Corinthians 3:17–18)

The reason I started to write this story as Kyloon was because it was much easier to tell a story about another person rather than take ownership of what truly happened to me. As my story proceeded and took form, I began to understand that Kyloon was not, of course, another person, but another entity within me who wanted to tell her story. I used Kyloon because it was the name a Chinese Christian man I knew in Ecuador used to call me with adoration and affection. It was at that time that I learned to truly love myself with my whole heart, and to me, the name Kyloon means love, honor, and respect.

My real name is Karen, but Kyloon is very much a part of me. If it had not been for Kyloon, I would not be telling this story. It was because of her courage and desire to be heard that I am able to tell you about the rest of the story. Karen has been living in shame, fear, and with all the other monsters mentioned earlier for too long.

My dream is to have a life I can be proud of. Here is the story of Karen's—*my*—recovery.

Steps to Recovery

Grief was one of the first emotions I allowed myself to feel. I almost didn't allow myself that luxury, but one of my colleagues made me go home and not return to school for three days after my mother died. This teacher took care of all my meetings and classes. After going to see my family after the death of my mother, I realized how little I thought of myself if I would not even have allowed myself time to mourn the loss of a parent.

Through professional help, I have a schedule each week to accomplish three or four achievable tasks that will help me move forward in my quest toward a more self-fulfilled life. Such a task would be to invite a friend to my home. This was scary because I had isolated myself from others for so many years. However, I anticipate having the emotions of joy, peace, and happiness present in my life once again.

When I first told my husband of my intent to divorce him, and to follow through with it this time, the news was not taken well. He reverted to childish behavior. I could have tolerated his reaction behavior, but a planned trip to go bowling with our daughter had to be cancelled when she found him in his recliner in a prenatal position bawling his eyes out. One might be touched by his sentimentality, but the divorce was not news to him. He knew about it, but thought that he might be able to change my mind. His emotional ties were about to be broken, and this was very threatening to him. Abusive people need others to stand by them.

My husband moved out only after he was able to convince me that a separation was far better than a divorce. He was then able to stay on my health insurance.

"Why be hasty in making a quick decision," he told me.

After agonizing over the decision to divorce him, my husband was now asking me to change my mind with the idea of only a separation. I agreed. He always could convince me to do anything. Why? Fear, I believe.

Confusion is another very strong emotion that kept crawling up. It could almost fit the category of monster. As long as my husband could keep me hoping for a positive change, the longer he could have control of the situation. These thoughts rolled around in my mind along with the ones that told me I had to take control myself.

I had been separated from my husband for less than a month when I began to experience a peeling of layers of emotions; these are often referred to as *protective layers*. I had begun to emerge from the depths of my soul to rediscover my true identity. The peeling of layers might not appear to be a very difficult or lengthy process for some, but these perceptions are wrong. For me, the process will most likely be long and often painful. At least, this is what I am expecting. I have stuffed my emotions for so long, I believe the uncovering and letting go will be long, too, but I'm ready for the challenge.

As in any other addiction, I had been caught up in the cycles of fear, anger, self-worthlessness, and no hope of affection. I was asked by a counselor, just after my first year of marriage, "Why do you allow your husband to be mean to you?"

Eventually, I realized the answer was within myself, not from others or because of others.

I became angry with the counselor for asking such a question. "I *wasn't* making him angry, he just *was!*"

Truly, I did not understand the depth of that question. Then I began asking myself why I had allowed myself to be verbally berated and humiliated over and over again. That was the big question. My recovery and healing depended on finding that answer.

Wherefore he saith, Awake thou that sleepest, and arise from the dead, and Christ shall give thee light. (Ephesians 5:14 KJV)

Here are some circumstances and examples I wrote about in my journal while searching for the answer.

Sense of no self-worth. Right at the end of school, I wanted to hold a barbeque at my house as a thank-you for all the help and love I had received during my first year. I wrote up an invitation, but couldn't hand it out. I was afraid. What if people didn't want to come? What if they felt that I was crazy to think they would *want* to come? I asked a friend at school and explained my fears. He told me to get over it and just ask. "Too bad what they think!" was his response to my paranoia. He smiled and reassured me. The party was a success.

Self-doubt of intelligence and ability. I had the responsibility of paying the mortgage after my husband moved out. With the existing mortgage payment amount, I would not be able to pay all the bills. With these thoughts, I went to the bank to take out my portion of the money from the savings account. I felt as if I was stealing money from the bank. More guilt! My financial advisor convinced me to only invest part of the money in the mortgage and save the rest in case of an emergency. With his advice, I recalibrated my mortgage, invested in a money market account, and became somewhat independent with my money.

All this was a new concept for me. Even though when I was married I had my own accounts, I was too scared to spend any of my money. My husband had heard my financial advice, but ultimately, he controlled the money. He made the final decisions. This privilege to have a say in my finances was new to me. As I approached my financial advisor's door for my initial meeting, my stomach was in knots and my hands were shaking. *Could I possibly be smart enough to do all this? Can I really manage my own money?* Doubts like these filled my head time and time again. I had to say to myself that I could handle whatever came my way.

I often found myself thinking, *Wouldn't Kyloon be fearless and proud of her successes?* Kyloon was never afraid of a challenge.

Didn't she travel the world by herself and live to tell about it? Many times I thought about how fearless I used to be. I wondered if that really was true. Most likely I had fears at that time, but had them under control. Kyloon, the adventurous, emotional, sensitive, and empathetic side of me, now wanted to be heard.

Fear of physical disability. I am a survivor. At an early age, I decided that I would not allow my disabilities to affect my life, even if they had to be denied. My paralyzed left hand was the easiest to overcome. I can't remember what it was like to have a fully functioning left hand, so adjustments have been as normal as if it was fully functioning. Memory loss, confusion, and epilepsy, all due to the brain damage, were a lot harder to dismiss. These malfunctions were also harder to hide from the outside world, as well as from myself. The Kyloon part of me had to survive and she would do what she had to do.

Not long ago, I had to pass a state exam in reading, writing, and math in order to get my conditional teaching certification. I had never tested well. Recall was difficult for me, especially in reading and in writing. Brain damage was located on the right side of the brain where my head had gone through the windshield. One can only speculate if learning problems occurred as a result. For the state exam, I studied an average of ten hours a week from June 19 to August 4. The day of the exam, I thought I was well prepared. I had passed all the practice tests.

As I walked into the exam room, I was not prepared for the fluorescent lights. As soon as I walked in, the room started to vibrate. The words on the paper were moving all around. I had thought that if I studied hard enough and long enough, I could pass the test and no one would have to know I had disabilities, but I had not thought about the lights. Bright fluorescent lights are a problem for an epileptic.

The tests lasted three hours, with a half-hour break between the second and third tests. The first test was reading. I shaded my eyes from the lights and tried to concentrate on the written words to help me focus on comprehending the story and not on how the words were moving around. I finished the first test with ten minutes to review. The second test was a math exam, my strength. This test proved to be very difficult, with no time to review my answers. I was exhausted.

We had a thirty-minute break before tackling the writing exam. This proved to be the most difficult one. There were thirty-eight questions to answer in thirty minutes. I was brain-tired; I couldn't read, assess the mistakes, and write the answers on a score sheet in the allotted time. I had to guess to complete that section on the test. At the end of the test, we had thirty minutes to write an essay on a subject given by the administrators. This was not as hard, but my handwriting probably looked like a fifth grader's. I could hardly see the lines, but I completed the test.

The next few days were a blur to me. After the exam, I stayed home and cried for three days. I felt as if I was broken. Emotionally, I let out all the strain that had been built up prior to the test. I was so exhausted that anything physical put me back down on the couch to rest. After the third day, I began to feel physically and mentally stronger.

What had happened to me?
Why did I feel as though I had failed, even though I had
a good chance of passing the exams?

Fear of rejection. At that time, I had never been tenured into a school system. Schools would hire me and keep me up to the tenure mark. Then they would let me go without an adequate explanation. My evaluations were never in question up to then, but they would let me go. Each one of those school systems knew of my epilepsy. Did I appear as a risk to them?

Learning to love myself. After much contemplation, I realized that I didn't want my job to be in jeopardy, and hiding my disability would be the best option, but for whom?

Hiding fear of rejection kept me in captivity. I had to keep my emotions, bad or good, in hiding to succeed. Perhaps this is the key to why I allowed myself to remain in an abusive relationship. I needed to hide my emotions to keep the facade of happiness and success. However, there came a point where the Kyloon part of me could no longer be kept in hiding. She wanted to experience all the joy and happiness life had to offer, but she now had to learn to accept and love who she was with all her flaws. That is recovery.

These are only a few examples of my experiences over those first months of separation, and of the topics that I had to explore, relearn, accept, and, most importantly, love about myself. In the next chapters you will go on a journey with me as I explore these areas, and go on adventures that helped me build up those areas of weakness. In the end, I hope to show you that all is possible to those who believe.

Karen was captive to her fears. Even now, I am constantly being reminded of how many ways I struggled with the bondage of fear in all aspects of my life. Bondage brings feelings of inadequacy. Inadequacy brings fear. Fear is the root of all things negative in the core of one's being.

The Bible tells us, "You have not been given a spirit of fear, but of power and love and sound mind" (2 Timothy 1:7).

"Learning to partner with the spirit of Love requires you to become powerful." —Danny Silk, *Keep Your Love On: Connection, Communication & Boundaries*

I believe what I wrote, but I have learned something since I wrote that. The last time I called my counselor, I told her I had just fallen into my emotional hole again and could she fit me into her schedule?

She handed me a piece of paper as I walked through her door. I'll paraphrase what it stated:

Step 1. I'm walking down a busy street and I fall into this really big hole. I accidentally fall into it. It isn't my fault.

Step 2. I'm walking down the same street on another day. I see the hole, but I still fall into it. It isn't my fault.

Step 3. I'm walking down the street and I see the hole. I fall in this time, too, but I immediately get out. I know it *is* my fault. It has become a habit. I want to do something to prevent going in again.

Step 4. I see the big hole as I am walking down the same street, but this time I walk around it.

Step 5. I take another street.

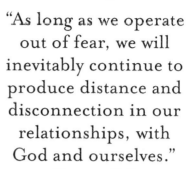

"As long as we operate out of fear, we will inevitably continue to produce distance and disconnection in our relationships, with God and ourselves."
— Danny Silk,
Keep Your Love On: Connection, Communication & Boundaries

I believe these are the phases of recovery. Our "holes" are habits of behavior that have been destructive to our lives. We continue with the same behaviors because they become comfortable. I still continue to fall into my hole, but each time I fall, I become a little wiser.

> *Bless them that curse you,*
> *and pray for them which despitefully use you.*
> (Luke 6:28)

My Journey

During the first months of my separation, I started to drink wine every night to cover the pain. It was no longer for pleasure, but to mask pain. I realized it when I had to go out in a storm to buy my bottle of wine. I did not want to end the day without that glass or two of wine. It relaxed me and helped me to sleep. That was true until it became a crutch, a friend, and then a need. I couldn't stop. It scared me. I had just watched my mother die from alcoholism. I attended my first AA meeting on November 6, 2007. This was just six months after my husband and I separated.

My friend at school had told me her story about how she had overcome her drinking problem. She had now been dry for twenty years and was now healthy and happy. I walked in on a Friday morning ready for school, but this day was different. Tears were flowing down my cheeks. I found her in her room preparing for the day, and I told her the truth. I told her I needed help. A huge weight lifted from my shoulders the moment I spoke those words. That week I went to my first AA meeting.

Breaking the habit of drinking every evening was difficult. I was an emotional drinker, and I knew that if I didn't stop, it could lead to a physical addiction. My mom had been an alcoholic. I did not want to die. I continued to attend meetings because I didn't trust myself. I was emotionally addicted to self-medicating, and I needed to stop.

That was a hole I did not want to fall into. I decided that if attending meetings could help me stop drinking, I would attend the meetings and admit that I was an alcoholic. I had a grandchild coming, and I wanted to make sure that my house was a safe place and a place of peace.

New Year's Eve proved to be most difficult. My daughter asked me if she could spend the evening with her sister and their father. I said of course, but my heart ached. I knew that I was going to be alone and this was not going to be good for me. I no longer worried about drinking, but just the thought of my family with my soon-to-be ex-husband and his girlfriend was not a happy thought. My brain started churning. *Who could I call?* I called my AA friend, and she said that there was a potluck dinner and a dance that night. She had not been planning to go, but she could take her kids with her and we could all go together. I immediately accepted her invitation. My husband and his girlfriend were running late and I had to leave fifteen minutes before they picked up my girls. Thank you, God!

It was rough on New Year's Day being alone. I called my neighbor, who I usual walked with at eight a.m. She was still asleep, but told me to come over and have coffee with her and then we would go for a walk. We spent the next couple hours in fellowship. The snow-covered back roads are breathtaking in Maine in the winter. Thank you, God!

That afternoon the pain emerged. My family was with a strange woman. My daughter called to say that they were going to the movies. I invited them for dinner, but they weren't sure because of the snowstorm that was expected that afternoon. I told them that I would cook anyway, and if they came a meal would be ready. I sobbed. I cried. I felt as though I had lost everyone. *Had I made a mistake?* Doubt was creeping in.

I called my sister, and with her experience of going through a divorce, I was hoping for a bit of wisdom. She reminded me of what I was standing up for. I was ending a verbally abusive relationship and I was dealing with a pregnant teenager who suffered from chronic depression, just like her father. She reminded me that my daughter was just trying to exist in this time of confusion. The existence of a whole family, even as play-acting, was comforting. My sister told me to paint or write to occupy my time. I decided to paint. I hadn't painted in almost twenty years. I was able to release my feelings on canvas, using colors as expressions and oils to spill out my feelings. A landscape of a lighthouse on the coast emerged. I would give it to my pregnant daughter and her fiancé as a house-warming gift. Thank you, God!

Peeling Is Productive, but Painful

This is my journey from codependency. This is a road that will take me the rest of my life to walk down. I must learn to love who I am, take care of myself, help others while not controlling them, accept my failures, and, most importantly, "let go and let God."

One of the greatest necessities to becoming whole after an abusive relationship is to allow the voices of all your parts to be heard. If you are like most abuse victims, you tend to stuff feelings and emotions in order to survive. We all want a normal life, so in order to achieve that, we must **stuff**.

If you have stuffed negative emotions or feelings away so that you didn't have to feel them, you've probably survived relatively happy, or at least it seemed that way for a while. These stuffed emotions/feelings need to be heard if you want to heal. I beg you not to try to do this without the assistance of a professional counselor. Once you have started the peeling process, you will believe that after each peeling you have completed the process, only to find another layer. For most of us, the abuse lasted many, many years, which requires as many layers to peel. Be patient with the process! I have experienced that my pain would only last one to three days for each layer, but the relief was immeasurable.

Here's an example. That first December after our separation, I wanted to purchase a Wii for my youngest daughter for Christmas. This was the one and only present she wanted, and I knew I could not afford a full-price version. I would find one on sale. I got a tip that Walmart had a shipment due in between eleven a.m. and two p.m. These were to be the discounted items. I had been unsuccessful so far, so I took the day off from school and arrived at the store at ten thirty. I stood next to the electronics counter. Two of the clerks told me that the UPS truck was not coming until twelve thirty, so I decided to do some shopping. When I returned to the counter at noon, I noticed that a sign had been put up on the counter: "One Wii per customer." This was a good sign. I approached the clerk to inquire about the arrival of the UPS truck, and the clerk looked confused.

"I'm sorry," he said. "The truck came at eleven. They are all sold."

I had either missed them or had I been sent away on purpose. *Maybe I was not good enough?* I went crazy and started to cry. I left the store. My next appointment was at three o'clock, and it was only twelve thirty. I made the conscious choice to *hear* the voice that was inside me crying so hard. I sobbed, a grieving sob from the center of my soul.

I asked myself, *"Why are you crying? It's okay to tell me. It's okay to feel as you do."*

I responded, **"I failed, as I have always failed throughout my whole life."**

I have failed as a daughter (black sheep of the family).

I have failed as a wife (divorce).

I have failed as a mother (my daughter had even told me so).

I cried for a total of six hours. I had to stop from three to six p.m. that day because I had a class, but I continued for the next two days.

Fortunately, I have a God who will carry me when I can't carry myself. I also have a counselor who will meet with me when I truly need her. My faith in the healing process gets me through when the pain is so severe.

When I met with my counselor, she asked me if that experience with crying and allowing my inner voice to be heard could be equated to falling in a hole. I said no, I was only allowing a voice to be heard that I had stuffed for too long.

A week later, I was driving to counseling when I realized that I had not repeatedly gone over in my mind what I was going to talk about in the session that day. I also realized that the last dart, one from my oldest daughter, hadn't hurt during the last few visits. The healing was in progress! This was the very first time I became conscious of how much healing had taken place.

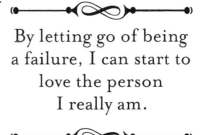

By letting go of being a failure, I can start to love the person I really am.

Another example of allowing a voice to be heard was after my first divorce court hearing. This was in January. I was physically sick with a nasty cold, I had a teacher observation the next day which I had forgotten about, and I was terribly stressed.

However, the court hearing went well. The judge gave my ex and me a month to work out an agreement outside the court. My ex did not like the fact that I requested spousal support beyond child-support years, but overall it went well. I went home and completed the paperwork for my observation the next day. In the morning, I pulled off the observation without any complications.

At least I thought I did. *Was doubt sneaking in again?*

I became disorientated, spacey, and almost confused. It was at the end of the school day, so I gathered all my school paraphernalia and left school as quickly as possible. When I got home, my youngest daughter wanted me to drive her to her friend's house to study. She was in her own world, just as any other fourteen-year-old would be, so she did not even notice that her mother was unstable. Thankfully, I was able to drive without incident. When I got back home, I slid onto the couch with a blanket over my head like a hoodie, and stared blankly at the TV for the next four hours. I reckon a gasket had blown in my brain somewhere. Perhaps it could be classified as a mini breakdown.

It was during this time that I talked to God. I was feeling as though I was ultra-vulnerable and open to attack. Who knows from whom, but I felt as though I was going to be attacked by someone and couldn't protect myself. I was scared.

Next, I talked to the voice within. Here was a little girl who was scared to death of being alone, of making mistakes, and of not being loved. I wanted to die, yet here I was, the adult and mother, and I was supposed to be the all-powerful and knowledgeable one.

Of course, I am not, but God is. He told me to relax. It was okay that I was feeling like that. I was just scared and that was normal after a divorce. *I felt so alone!* He told me to give myself some time and believe in Him when I couldn't trust in myself. His voice was heard and I gained strength from Him. Most importantly, I wasn't nuts. (Sometimes I really think I am!)

Peeling may be so painful, but it is so productive!

Let your inner voice be heard no matter how painful it may be. I only urge you not to try to do this without the help of a professional counselor. As the pain resurfaces, there will be times when you will think that it was better before, when you stuffed all those negative emotions/feelings. You must have faith that this pain won't last and healing will follow!

God loves you and so do I.

Knowing this, that the trying of your faith works patience.
(James 1:3)

Coming Out of Prison (No Self-Respect)

The whole process of an individual ending a verbally abusive relationship that lasted many years (mine was eighteen years) is like that of someone coming out of prison. You have no social skills, no self-esteem, and you really don't know how to conduct yourself in social situations outside the home. You are no longer the person you were before marriage, so you really don't *know* who you are. I imagine all divorcees have to go through this. It is a rediscovery of who you are.

Survivors of abuse have to learn to love themselves again. This is not always easy when you are constantly being reminded of your failures or shortcomings. For me, it is at my kitchen table that I am reminded of my failures. Yes, my kitchen table. I don't like to eat at it anymore because it still brings me to tears.

During my marriage, I often came home from work to prepare dinner and my husband would refuse to eat with us. He would separate himself from the family and eat at the kitchen counter much later, when he was calmed down from the day. Even when I prepared his favorite meals, he would not sit down with us. This left me with a feeling of unworthiness. You never knew what mood he would be in. More often than not, the girls and I ate alone at the table, or we would eat in the living room.

A few years later, when I invited my daughter and her fiancé to my house for dinner to tell them of my decision not to let them live with me, I lost my daughter's respect while sitting at that table.

A friend of mine helped me through this dilemma. He helped me stand up on my own and respect myself. By respecting myself, I can let go more easily. Being the mother of a pregnant teenager who would not allow me to help was very painful. I needed to let go and wait until she came back; I would be here.

I needed to learn how to be stronger and self-directed. If I could do this, I hoped and prayed I would gain some respect from my daughters. I needed to take the spotlight off of them and concentrate on me.

I prayed, "God, direct my path. Guide me according to Your will. Help me to be the best I can be. I give You all of my life."

I kept telling myself to let go, but I never seemed to accomplish it. A few years ago, my younger sister and I were talking about her husband and his strong family values. It just started to click. I have very strong family values, too, but was never able to fulfill them with my husband. Due to his past, he had under developed family values. I tried and tried, but never succeeded. I am beginning to see why I couldn't let go without my heart being ripped out. It isn't me.

As I became more and more aware of how my inner sub-consciousness worked, the easier it was for me to love myself where I was and let go of the past.

As I did my peeling of the layers of fear, guilt, doubt, insecurity, and dread, I found that Karen was BROKEN. After all that work of painful peeling, I found a broken person underneath. I was angry, grief-stricken, frightened, and sad. The emotions were overwhelming. How could this be? I had spent so much time and pain peeling the layers only to find my genuine self was a broken person. Well, let me tell you, there is hope. This broken person can heal!

Healing the broken person inside is not a quick, easy process, nor is it painless. I read somewhere, "The only way around pain is through it." That is so true. If we continually try to go around it, we still carry it. If we go through it, we can let it go.

How do I let go of the pain of being told that I am to blame for my husband's insanity?

How do I let go of the pain of being told I am to blame for my daughter's misery?

64

How do I let go of the pain of knowing that my other daughter blames me for her sister's misery?

All I know is that I have to let go for my *own* sanity's sake. Otherwise, I will die.

Wisdom Nuggets

"Many today are struggling to heal themselves from their sicknesses, diseases, mental dysfunctions, and addictions. I want to announce to you today that our part is to *receive* forgiveness from Jesus and to believe that we are forgiven every single day. The more forgiveness-conscious we are, the more easily we will experience healing and liberty from every bodily ailment, mental oppression, and destructive habit." -**Joseph Prince Ministries, Grace Inspirations**

"By focusing on the goodness of God and waiting, hoping, and expecting Him to encourage you and fill you with His peace and joy, you can overcome negative thoughts that drag you down. Think and speak positively. Begin believing right now that you are about to see God's goodness in your life. Wait, hope, and expect His blessings to be abundant in your life." —**Kanna**

"God's number one goal with us is connection, and nothing, pain nor death, will prevent Him from moving towards us and responding in Love." -**Danny Silk,** *Keep Your Love On: Connection, Communication & Boundaries*

Questions to Ponder and Journal About

Have you been able to peel back layers of your "monsters"?
What monsters did you discover?
Who did you discover you are?
Do you feel you are broken, too? Explain.
What feelings did you discover that you might have buried?
Can you love yourself through these new emotions?
Can you love your new broken self with all its flaws and weaknesses?

Read Luke 4:18.

What did Jesus say He was sent to do?

Is this available to you?

Thank God right now for what He is doing and going to do in your life.

Pray: *Create in me a clean heart so that I may be of service to You.*

CHAPTER 5

FINDING ANSWERS

Finding the Right Help through Support Groups

There are support groups out there for people like me. The program is called Al-Anon. It is based on a twelve-step program that helps people achieve serenity and peace in their lives after losing their lives to someone else. Usually, the people they lost their lives to were abusive. Most people think of Al-Anon as just for partners of alcoholics, but it can be for any partner who has become codependent from years of caretaking. This caretaking might have been of an alcoholic, an emotionally or mentally disabled person, or anyone who needed physical or emotional support to function. Women, especially, take on this role. They were brought up to take care of all emotional needs except their own. This is a natural role for them as mothers, and they can easily get caught up in the caretaking role.

I had first started attending regular AA meetings in the fall of 2008 because of my drinking. I was scared. I know God brought me there to hear about the twelve-step program. As I listened to the members' stories, I knew I needed help. With each meeting, the help I needed became more and more apparent. I needed to change my thinking. It was how I thought about and held on to things that was wrong. I knew the twelve steps could help me, but

I felt I was in the wrong place. Hadn't I been drinking? Wasn't my mom an alcoholic?

I turned to my counselor for help, and she pointed out that my primary problem was **codependency**. If I had continued drinking, I most likely would have gotten addicted. Drinking was prevalent in my family. This is a pattern of behaviors that I really must be careful of, even now.

I attended my first Al-Anon meeting in February, 2009. Immediately, I knew that this was a better fit for me. You must find the right fit for yourself. Go out and attend these different self help meetings and try them out. Finding support to rebuild yourself is important in your recovery.

My first meeting was in a group that supported women from abusive relationships. I attended one meeting and immediately fell into my emotional hole. I did not find reliving the experiences helpful. I needed someone to help my brain stop thinking negative thoughts! My next meeting was the AA meeting. It was here that I learned about the twelve-step program, which could help me with my thought processes; it helped me to stop drinking to cover my pain, and I learned about the effects of alcoholism. I attended church every week and found that there I could release the pain I had uncovered during the week. I could do this because the atmosphere of love in church gave me a sense of security. God heard my cries and took my burdens away.

At the Al-Anon meetings, I could go through the Twelve Steps and deal with my codependency. I always have the option to go back to AA meetings if I wanted or needed to, but I have not wanted to return to drinking emotionally. I don't want to go back there. I am keeping my sobriety because I feel good and believe that for me this is the best decision. Why play with fire?

You might ask, "What are these steps you're talking about?" The Twelve Steps are a set of principles, spiritual in nature, which, if practiced as a way of life, can expel an obsession (drinking, caretaking, etc.), and enable the sufferer to become happily and usefully whole. Thousands of people have found in these steps a way to a happy and effective way of living, whether alcoholics or not.

AA and Al-Anon's Twelve Steps

1. We admitted we were powerless over alcohol [any obsession]—that our lives had become unmanageable.
2. Came to believe that a Power greater than ourselves could restore us to sanity.
3. Made a decision to turn our will and our lives over to the care of God *as we understood Him.*
4. Made a searching and fearless moral inventory of ourselves.
5. Admitted to God, to ourselves, and to another human being the exact nature of our wrongs.
6. Were entirely ready to have God remove all these defects of character.
7. Humbly asked Him to remove our shortcomings.
8. Made a list of all persons we have harmed, and became willing to make amends to them all.
9. Made direct amends to such people wherever possible, except when to do so would injure them or others.
10. Continued to take personal inventory and when we were wrong promptly admitted it.
11. Sought through prayer and meditation to improve our conscious contact with God *as we understood Him*, praying only for knowledge of His will for us and the power to carry that out.
12. Having had a spiritual awakening as the result of these Steps, we tried to carry this message to alcoholics [codependents], and to practice these principles in all our affairs.

Working the Steps/Walking Down a Different Road

Learning how to train your mind to think differently is a tedious process because your mind wants to go back to the way it used to think. I often have to ask God to help me let go of negative thoughts and destructive thought patterns.

My younger daughter said it perfectly, "Mom, you think all the bad things are happening to you. You are gossiping with your friends about my sister and her fiancé and about how bad they are. You just need attention for yourself."

This was her perception, but I looked into it for truth. I had been talking to a friend who is a psychologist. She understands the dynamics of relationships and the consequences of certain behaviors. My conversation could easily have been looked upon as gossip with no regard for those I was speaking of. What was my true reason for talking to her? *I* wanted to be heard. *I* was hurt. *I* had been excluded from my daughter's life as some sort of punishment, and *I* was angry. That was the truth.

I couldn't sleep that night after my young daughter, at the age of fourteen, had confronted me. I apologized. I told her the next morning that I had been hurt by not being allowed to join them that New Year's weekend, and had forgotten to believe in her sister and her fiancé, no matter the situation they were in. I thanked her for reminding me to believe in them. Since that talk, our relationship has been less strained in the house. That is "working the Steps."

I even contemplated the true reason why I am constantly in the process of telling my story. My primary purpose was to help document what was happening to me in the household. Due to the nature of my ex's behavior, I often was unaware of the darts flying at me until the damage was already done. Writing down events helped me to digest the truth. As I continued to write, I realized that I might be able to help someone else in my position. Through the pain, I know I have a purpose. It really helps me to hang on when I don't have the strength to do so.

I have my court case today. There are a few issues I want to write about because they are heavy on my mind. Writing helps me clear my mind. Below is a list of my concerns and worries.

1. *Ex won't agree to alimony payments.*
2. *He believes that he shouldn't pay.*
3. *He told me that my daughter disrespects me because I am asking him for alimony payments.*

4. *He is using her to make me feel guilty (old tactic).*
5. *He is unable to make a decision regarding his money.*
6. *He is making the courts make the decision. (This could be good because then he couldn't blame me.)*
7. *He will blame me anyway for having to pay the courts.*
8. *I feel as though I shouldn't have asked for alimony. If I only asked for child support, we could have agreed. (doubt)*
9. *If I had allowed my daughter and her fiancé to live with me, I would never have lost their respect. (doubt)*
10. *Standing up for myself is a new behavior for me. I feel so guilty.*
11. *I feel as though I am the bad guy if I stand up for myself and have my voice heard. This is what I learned throughout my marriage. If I ever did in the past, I was put down. Refer back to the [journal] entry when I tried to communicate with him about his behavior and the effects on the family.*
12. *I hope and pray that God's will be done today in the courts. (My ex will try to make me feel guilty.)*

My ex is a troubled individual. He really has a kind heart and tries so hard to be a good person. Everyone enjoys his company. No one would ever believe me about the darts that flew on a regular basis at home. He never displayed the anger monster outside the home. His outside manner was of one who was articulate, funny, intelligent, and cute. His dimples and smile always won the hearts of the people he smiled upon. His monster hid within and emerged only when he felt safe at home (Classic passive/aggressive communicator).

It was the monster inside that I tried to tame for the eighteen years of our marriage. It was his monster that he was running away from again. I finally got it! I had no control over helping him. I had to let go of him and his monsters for my sanity's sake. I pray and hope that someday he will have the guts and strength to face his monsters and conquer them (Classic passive communicator and rescuer).

The court case went well. My psychologist friend and I prayed before the appointed time of our meeting, "God, your will be done." My ex offered to pay a lesser amount of spousal support. I agreed. Thank you, God.

I called my ex and told him I wanted to meet his significant other. He responded that he would ask her if she wanted to. I stated that that was not an option. If she was spending so much time with my kids, I wanted to meet her face to face. I told him that I would be at their apartment in the afternoon while both kids were away.

I arrived at the apartment only to have my younger daughter run out and say, "You can't come in! This will make her feel uncomfortable."

I told my child that it was alright because it was all prearranged. They both knew I was coming. I walked in and both kids were sitting on the floor with their backs to me. I had walked into a home where I was definitely not welcome. It was very uncomfortable. My ex's girlfriend never got up or asked me to take off my coat. I sat down and listened to a conversation that I was not a part of. My oldest daughter never looked me in the eyes, and my younger daughter kept giving me the eyes that said I must leave. My ex just ignored me. After a while, I left, saying that it had been a pleasure to meet her.

I completely broke apart as I drove down the street. I felt as if I had lost my whole family. I cried, moaned, sobbed, and thought that this was the moment that I really would die. Then I thought, *Perhaps today is the day that I should hear my kids cry. Have I been crying so long and so hard that I have not been able to hear my children cry?*

My older daughter would not talk to me or associate with me, yet she spent time with her dad. Her dad wanted to take her and her fiancé into his apartment even after we had decided that the best decision for them was to let them make it on their own. I had lost the respect of my daughter. She wouldn't even look at me. I searched and searched for the truth. I died a million deaths with these thoughts.

Did I do something wrong?

Was I such a bad person that she would not want to associate with me?

Did my drinking scare her?

Was I too self-absorbed to hear her cries?

After attending many Al-Anon meetings, I came to understand the nature of the beast that lives within me. It is a form of insanity that results from living with the disease of alcoholism. As the codependent, I am crazier than the alcoholic. I've reviewed what I have written so far, only to confirm my situation. The only difference is that now I know I am not alone and that there is a recovery program that can restore my sanity. I have made progress. Karen is progressively moving from powerless to powerful.

I now can look at my behavior and know when I am overreacting, step back, and pray. It is not easy for me. A woman I met at Al-Anon became my sponsor, and she has been taking me through the steps.

It's April 4th and I'm only on Step 2 since February. I have a feeling that this recovery for me is going to be a long process, to rid me of the old thinking behaviors and replace them with much healthier ones.

My younger daughter has been my rock. She often tells me right away when I'm acting out of line. It often revolves around her sister and my desire to be part of their lives. Her sister is still very angry at me. I must look within and ask why.

As a codependent, I have a tendency to focus only on my own reactions. I need to let go and let God handle all situations that are out of my control. It goes back to the Serenity Prayer, which states, **God grant me the serenity to accept the things I cannot change, the courage to change the things I can, and the wisdom to know the difference.**

Powerless = Powerful

I pray, "God help me to let go of every situation and person that I've tried to control in the past." When I let them go, God can work in their lives to do His will. When I'm always interfering, I prevent God from doing His thing. The loving thing to do on my part is to let go. When I'm letting go, I am getting better. Once I'm better, others can depend on me.

I have made progress, but I still hurt. It hurts to let go. Each time I let go, I see God working His miracles. I know I will not see those miracles if I interfere in His work.

My sponsor told me to write a list of all the times in my life that I felt powerless.

I felt powerless because of my accident at the age of eleven. I had to learn how to walk again. I was very weak and feeble for about a year, which made me different from my peers.

Walking with God has shown me that the more I try to play god and interfere in His work, the longer it takes for the prayers to be answered. If I get out of the way and trust Him, miracles happen.

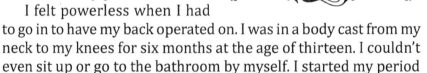

I felt powerless when I had to go in to have my back operated on. I was in a body cast from my neck to my knees for six months at the age of thirteen. I couldn't even sit up or go to the bathroom by myself. I started my period during those six months in the cast.

I felt powerless because once I got out of my cast, I was out of the social loop and had a difficult time socially from the age of fourteen to sixteen.

I felt powerless because I was raped at the age of fourteen.

I felt powerless because from the age of eighteen to twenty-one during college, I gained a lot of weight—50 pounds! Although I gave my life to the Lord at the age of nineteen in the Canary Islands, I had no one to mentor me to help grow in the Lord.

I felt powerless because from age twenty-one to twenty-six, I traveled the world alone, teaching and searching for an answer to who I was.

I felt powerless between the ages of twenty-six and thirty-two because I was in search of a husband back in the States.

I felt powerless because of my seizures. It wasn't until I was forty-five that I got the medicine to control my type of seizures. My seizures only occurred when I was sleeping, and doctors gave me medicine that drugged me during the day. I finally saw a specialist who gave me medicine just for nighttime and the grand mal seizures stopped! From eighteen until forty-five years old, I suffered grand mal seizures a few times a year. I felt powerless that whole time.

I felt powerless at the age of thirty-two when I married my husband. Within the first year, I was in counseling asking why someone would be so mean to another being.

I felt powerless from the ages of thirty-two to fifty-two because I was married to a man who was very verbally abusive to me when he was unhappy, which was most of the time. During my entire marriage, I felt powerless.

I felt powerless because after the separation from my husband in 2007, I began the process of peeling the layers of negative emotions. I was in therapy. The process was long and hard.

I felt powerless when only four months after the separation, I found out about his girlfriend. The pain was so severe that I was drinking two or three glasses of wine a night to deal with the pain.

I felt powerless because my daughter's boyfriend was living at my house during the summer helping me with the upkeep until he could find a place to live. In the meantime, I got the news that she was pregnant. I found out that he was still married to his ex and was driving without insurance. I really liked the guy, but I didn't want to care for another male who couldn't take care of himself. I didn't want my daughter to have to go through the same thing I did. There was unrest in the house. I can't explain it other than there was something spiritually wrong and it filled the house, so I told him to leave. My daughter walked out, too, and that was the last time I had any civil respect from her even after I apologized about the way I had told him to leave.

I felt powerless because when my daughter and her fiancé moved out of my house, they moved into their own two-room apartment. I had given them a month's rent and security deposit that they said they would eventually pay back. They were only there two months before they moved in with her father. Now they only had to pay half the rent and they got a bigger place.

I felt powerless when I was paying for my ex's health insurance while he supported his girlfriend and bought a house for her. He kept the apartment where he let my daughter live with her boyfriend, so he could have a place to stay during the week because the drive to his girlfriend's was an hour and half away from work. I felt extremely powerless.

I felt powerless when, after the year of counseling and removing the many emotional layers that I had buried, I realized that I was broken within.

I felt powerless when I thought there was no hope for me. I had lost the respect of my older daughter; I feared losing my youngest daughter to this new woman; my social skills were a wreck. I had lived in fear for so long that I had (and still have) a hard time making friends. It all appeared hopeless.

I am trying to be honest with myself so that I can heal. I feel alone. I could have called someone tonight, but I'd rather be alone. I'm cleaning house, resting, and writing. I can paint or read, take a tub. I've been in class all day and am looking forward to a quiet evening. I can go to a Big Book meeting tomorrow morning at 8 in Belfast and still make church. I think I will. I also have a paper to write. I just wish I had some company—a male companion to watch TV with and enjoy each other's company. God knows who that is. I must be patient with myself and let Him finish the work that He started to do in me and also in the person He is preparing.

The Anger Issue

I have to admit that I have been feeling anger lately. It's a strange and new feeling for me, as I have never allowed myself to feel this emotion, which was the emotion that was so destructive to my life. **I feel guilty for feeling angry about the mistreatment that befell my existence.** *I feel angry that my ex has told my daughter that it's all right to be angry at [her] mom. He never says things outright, but through his behaviors, he implies things. He makes excuses for her behavior. The behaviors I took years to mold, he is undoing. His behavior implies that he cares, yet in the past, when I was there, he couldn't care about the kids or their schedules. Now he is there to take care of it all, making me look as though I don't care. He is settling down with another women, and the kids look at them as if they are happy and have it together. I plug along working the steps and cleaning out the baggage of my own basement, years of pain and fear. I don't get it! Perhaps I am angry because he appears to be happy. Perhaps I am angry because he is not taking ownership in the disaster of [our] marriage. The kids think that I am crazy.*

Anger is an emotion that I do not want to waste my time and energy on. I believe that if I rest my mind on anger, I will not be able to hear the messages from God. Many times, His voice is like a whisper and I have to keep a keen ear to the wind to hear. If my mind is clouded with negative emotions, I will miss a message meant for me alone.

I have forgiven my ex. He was troubled in his heart and mind and I could not expect him to respond as if he wasn't. I needed to love him where he was at, and allow him to take his own journey with God. *(Example of letting go and letting God!)*

As for my daughter, who was going through her own journey, I had to be patient with her, too. The best thing I could do for her at that time was to love and support her from a distance. At first, this distance was killing me. I felt rejected and hurt that I could not be a part of her life. This was very selfish of me. She was hurt and lost, trying to make sense of the situation she had found herself in. I had to give her all the love I could send her from a distance. When she was ready, she would call. *(Strength and patience that only comes from the Lord.)*

Victim to Victor

These questions helped me answer a big question in my heart: Was I playing a victim or a victor?

1. What am I responding to?
I have been responding to my negative emotions, allowing them to rule my life. This has been selfish, because it has prevented me from helping others.

2. Have I told the truth to myself?
No, I have wanted to believe that I was the victim, not the person reacting.

3. Have I told the truth to others?
No. Often I share my woes with others, which is selfish. This has only brought them down rather than lift them up.

4. What is my vision?
My prayer is for a clean heart. I have tried to give God my fears, pains, resentments, and regrets, not always successfully.

5. What am I expecting of myself?
I am expecting to be patient with myself. Each day is a new day to grow and heal.

6. What is my intention?
My intention is to love again with a pure heart.

7. Can I love myself no matter what happens?
I hope and pray that I can rid myself of all self-hatred and unworthiness. I want to love my past experiences because they have made me who I am.

8. Can I love others no matter what they do?

I am learning how to do this. I become angry and impatient with others when they don't live up to my expectations. I know this is selfish of me.

Here is a letter that I wrote to my older sister searching for answers:

I felt like writing, so I'm writing to [you] about the events of my heart. It has been a quiet few days and time for me to reflect on the past. I saw my sponsor from Al-Anon on Wednesday and she informed me that I haven't even made it beyond the first Step, which is accepting the fact that I am powerless over other people and how they react or think. Here I was thinking I was on to Step 4. The first three Steps are really learning how to change your thought patterns and give everything over to God. I had everything about the spiritual aspect under control, but not my thought patterns. When she spoke the word "powerless," I finally got it. Since then, I have been able to detach from my ex and my oldest daughter in my unhealthy thoughts. The pain stopped.

Yesterday I was in a state of exhaustion. I rested and was quiet. This morning I feel empty, but healthier. I feel I am ready to move on. My ex stopped by yesterday and helped me get all the summer furniture out. I, on the other hand, gave him the paperwork he needed to buy a house. It didn't hurt. I felt distant, but friendly. Odd! I guess I'm moving on with my life. Not any too soon, with the baby coming!

I also feel that when I am ready, another husband will be there. This time, I won't have to pursue or even try; that man will give me strength, rather than sucking it from me. When I am ready, so will he be. So, I have my house, my younger daughter, and my older daughter with a baby on the way. I think I will keep busy until that happens. Thanks for listening.

Over the next weekend I struggled with the word "powerless," but what I was really struggling with was what I was powerless over. I gave my ex and my oldest daughter up to God one more time. I felt empty because I felt that I was giving up any kind of influence in their lives. The emptiness was because I *was* empty. I was depressed, alone, and useless.

When I let go of the stuff I don't want, God can fill me up even more abundantly with His power and love. I admitted that I am powerless over my own thinking and can only let go with the power from God.

In the middle of the night, God spoke to me and told me to ask Him to fill me up.

You might wonder what type of thinking could be so damaging. In my case, it was thinking that if I just changed *my* behaviors, I would

get a different result from my family. I tried every conceivable action to produce a positive reaction from both my ex and my oldest daughter, but all my actions did was irritate them more. Then I thought that if I just offered my help, became a better mother, wife, and individual, they would love me more. These are a few of the insane, obsessive thoughts that continually ran through my mind. These are very typical thoughts for the loved one of an alcoholic, emotionally abusive partner. I became codependent and addicted to the abuser.

Removing Negative Thoughts

Once I decided to do the Steps and get a sponsor, I knew that my Lord would honor my request, and I knew I could become a totally healed and productive person. I could love without needing to be loved back. My goal was to love unconditionally without the obsessive need to be acknowledged or taken care of. I wanted to love from the heart. I now knew, God would provide what I needed.

The summer of 2008 was one of extreme growth for me. I examined my heart and found all the fears, resentments, and negative thoughts that bound me and kept me from being free. I spent one whole weekend with two spiritual friends who helped me see the nature of this truth.

They helped me to see that all people are a combination of body, soul, and spirit. These are the three natures of mankind. The body is the flesh, the soul is a person's thoughts and emotions, conscious and unconscious, and the spirit is that part that is inherent only in humans. That spirit can be born again of God.

The soul of a person can become very clouded with negative thoughts and emotions as a result of life's experiences. We often hide these experiences in the recesses of our hearts so that we don't have to feel the pain they bring upon us. Once we have hidden bad, hurtful episodes of our lives away, they become like a sore. At first, they do not bother us, but eventually, if left untreated, they will fester and become infected, only to erupt in unexpected places and times.

And the very God of peace sanctify you wholly; and [I pray God] your whole spirit and soul and body be preserved blameless unto the coming of our Lord Jesus Christ.
(1 Thessalonians 5:23)

That weekend, my two friends and I traveled to visit different parts of the state that we had never seen before. We ended up having lunch in the town where my ex and his girlfriend had bought their house. I sat in the restaurant and started to cry. The pain was very intense, located directly in my heart. I explained to my friends what this town was and how it was affecting me.

The pain felt as though I had been truly rejected by the person whom I had loved and honored. I felt abandoned and cast out by him because I was not good enough.

When I told them this, one of them told me to face my pain—and then she stated, "You left him because it was a toxic relationship. You let him go so that he could face himself and his own problems. You left him because you no longer wanted to be the recipient of his anger. It was your choice to stay with him as long you did. He never tied you down and told you that you couldn't leave. It was your choice then and it is your choice now. The pain of rejection is a lie."

I truly appreciated the bluntness of my friend who had my best interest at heart.

The truth is I have been carrying the lie of rejection since childhood. The accident had left me scarred and scared that I was not good enough. The fear of abandonment resulted from believing I was not good enough. That was a lie locked up in my heart because it was too painful to face, but I faced it in the town my ex had moved to while I sat in that restaurant. The proximity—knowing that their house was nearby—was too much for me to hide that pain. My friend, who had the wisdom to make me face it and turn the lie around to the truth, helped me find the healing, liberty, and awareness that I needed. This removed the hold that lie had on me in that area. I immediately felt cleaner, lighter, and more at peace.

How many more layers of fear and resentment are beneath the surface of my heart? I pray on a daily basis that these layers will be revealed to me and that I will be able to face them and turn them around when they appear. With a cleaner heart and less pain in my soul, I can be used more by God for His purpose.

Faithful [is] he that calleth you, who also will do [it].
(1 Thessalonians 5:24 KJV)

I had another life-changing experience when I realized that I had to acknowledge not only the abandonment I felt, but the rejection, too. In August of that same year, I had been working on the topic of the fears that I had felt since childhood and where they were now. I did not have to look hard for the answer to that one. They were located in the depths of my heart, hidden so no one (including me) could see or feel them—or at least that's what I had thought. Here is another story that made me realize I had a voice within that needed to be heard.

My ex and his girlfriend, my two daughters, and my grandson were all going to visit his relatives, so they could meet his new girlfriend. He had been with her for more than a year at that point. I was glad he was taking her because his sister really wanted to meet them all. My brain said one thing while my heart felt another: rejection! *Will the negative thinking ever stop?*

That same year, my younger daughter turned fourteen, I had a cancerous mole removed from my back, tendonitis in my shoulder, and three open, bleeding cold sores on my lower lip. Negative thoughts bombarded my mind 24/7! Negative thoughts about my ex would not leave my head day or night, every waking moment. In addition, I was hosting two Chinese girls that week, which added to the pressure. Then my daughter pulled a stunt that broke my trust with her.

In the midst of the clamor that was trying to drive me crazy, I realized that the noise I was experiencing all around me was **anger**, an emotion that had been repressed for nearly twenty years. Once I recognized what it was, I started to laugh. I laughed out loud in my house when I was all alone. One would have thought I was a madwoman!

This is anger? I thought. *No wonder I didn't want to feel it. But suddenly I realized the noise had stopped! Why?*

Following is a Bible study that I wrote when looking for that answer.

Jesus says, "**Blessed are the poor in spirit**" (Matthew 5:3). That means no inner baggage (monsters) and no self-identification, but purely and simply walking in the spirit with God.

How do I overcome fear? "**And the Peace of God which surpasses all comprehension shall guard your hearts and your minds**" (Philippians 4:7).

To let go of all the "stuff and things of life" and give them to God I need to, "Be anxious for nothing, but in everything by prayer and supplication [repeated request by prayer] with thanksgiving let your requests be known to God" (Philippians 4:6).

What is negative thinking? Sin = Negative thinking. It is one of Satan's device to captivity. Examples we don't want to include are complaining and fault-finding (blaming).

"**Why do you look at the speck that is in your brother's eye, but do not notice the log that is in your own eye?**" (Luke 6:41). When I criticize or condemn another, it makes me feel bigger and superior. The **ego** loves to complain and feel resentful. It loves to feel that we are **right** and it enjoys making someone else **wrong**.

People become addicted to pain. The **ego** feeds on all negative food to live. Being a victim is an addiction! *How do I stop my sick and perverted ego?* **Forgiveness,** because another word for non-reaction is forgiveness. Jesus taught us to love and forgive even our enemies. **"Love your enemies and do good and lend, expecting nothing in return: and your reward will be great and you will be sons of the Most High"** (Luke 6:35-38).

In 2 Corinthians 2.5-8, Paul was writing to the church to forgive someone who had done him wrong, but who was remorseful. Forgive him and love him because his remorse is punishment enough. I am to forgive him and comfort him.

In 2 Corinthians 2:10-11, it says, **"But one whom you forgive anything, I forgive also; for indeed what I have forgiven, if I have forgiven anything, I did it for your sakes in the presence of Christ, so that no advantage would be taken of us by Satan, for we are not ignorant of his schemes."** Satan loves us to believe his lies.

Wisdom Nuggets

Cleansing your mind from negative thinking allows you to hear God's voice.

Listen to your thoughts and accept them as valid.

Love yourself and then change your thoughts to positive thoughts of thanksgiving through the Word.

Give all your thoughts to God through prayer and meditation (quiet time with God).

Give your actions to God so that you can be used as an ambassador of Christ.

To build healthy relationships, one must learn how to become an assertive communicator, removing oneself from the role of victim, bad guy or rescuer.

"One must move from control to self-control, make a goal of distance to connectlon and from fear to love." -Danny Silk, *Keep Your Love On: Connection, Communication & Boundaries*

Questions to Ponder and Journal About

List all the things that you feel powerless about, starting from your earliest memories of childhood to the present.
What are you responding to?
Have you told the truth to yourself?
Have you told the truth to others?
What is your vision?
What are you expecting of yourself?
What is your intention?
Can you love yourself no matter what happens?
Can you love others no matter what they do?
What are your negative voices?
What are they trying to tell you?

Pray: *Create in me a clean heart so that I may be of service to You.*

CHAPTER 6

KAREN, KYLOON, AND ME

The Child Within Is Found, Reunited, and Heard

How can I feel rejected when we are divorced
and I don't want to go back to him?
Who is talking or feeling that way?

I wanted to find out. One time, soon after the divorce, in the middle of the night I woke up to feel the child within my heart crying. I literally held my hand to my heart and told her I would take care of her.

I called my counselor early and met with her that very next morning. We then had the experience of meeting the little girl. This little girl, who had been locked up inside me for forty-one years, decided it was time to leave her prison. Did she feel a sense of security or even a newfound sense of independence? I believe she felt that her host, Karen, was healed enough to allow her child's voice to be heard.

He healeth the broken in heart, and bindeth up their wounds.
(Psalm 147:3 KJV)

Sitting in the counseling room, I told my counselor my intention of letting the child out. I stood up and told the counselor that I needed a hug. Tears were running down my face. A frightened child emerged, crying as we hugged. Words like, "I was so scared, I was so alone," came out of my mouth. I, Karen, also said, "She is so dynamic." The whole process took about two minutes.

Teary-eyed, my counselor said, "Thank you for allowing me to be part of that experience."

"Who is this little girl? What is her name?" she asked me.

"Karen," I answered. "This is me as a child who didn't want to be seen. Everyone saw Kyloon, the strong one, who could overcome everything, but Karen was the frightened little girl who wasn't good enough."

My counselor had been working with me for the last year, uncovering the many layers. I would not have tried to reach the frightened, hurt child without her. Plus, the child within was so scared that she did not want to come out unprotected. She wanted to be with someone who understood her.

Karen, the frightened child, wanted to be heard. Following are some of the feelings that she had kept locked up inside herself for so long. She wanted to be heard in order to let them go.

- I am not good enough. I cannot walk straight as a result of the accident.
- I am not good enough. I cannot learn as well as my sisters.
- I am not good enough. I have a paralyzed hand that does not work.
- I am not good enough. I have seizures.
- I am not good enough. I am not pretty.
- I am not good enough. I am fat.
- I am not good enough. I cannot do anything well enough for my father.
- I am not good enough. I cannot ever match up to my father's acceptance of my sisters.
- I am not good enough. I'm stupid.
- I am not good enough. I don't know how to dress.
- I am not good enough. I don't know how to do anything right.

- I am not good enough. I cannot stand up to my ex's anger.
- I am not good enough. I cannot stand up to my daughter's anger.
- I am not good enough. I could not stand up to my father's anger.

These are some of the lies that I had told myself. These voices only separated me from God's truth of who I really am and who I really will become.

*For we are his workmanship, created in Christ Jesus unto good
works, which God hath before ordained that
we should walk in them.*
(Ephesians 2:10)

You might read this and think that I am schizophrenic, but I am not. The mind will play tricks on even the healthiest of brains, and make accommodations to make life easier for the host. In this story, that is **Me**. This is the story of how, Karen, the adult, got to meet, Kyloon, the survivor, and Me, the child, to become as one person, a whole being, integrated and conquering my fears together.

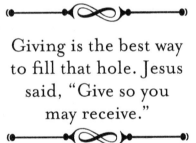

Giving is the best way to fill that hole. Jesus said, "Give so you may receive."

*He hath made everything beautiful in his time:
also he hath set the world in their heart,
so that no man can find out the work that God maketh
from the beginning to the end*
(Ecclesiastes 3:11)

That night, as I slept and awoke as I do every night, the little girl awoke with me. That night, I felt a giant hole in my chest. *Why a hole?* I asked myself. I realized that for the first time in many years, I didn't feel the pain that had occupied that portion of my heart. Now, I had to fill the hole with positive experiences.

Why are you cast down, O my soul,
and why are you disquieted within me?
Hope in God; for I shall again praise him, my help.
(Psalm 42:5)

"Be Blessed as God fills up the hole in your heart, those empty places, that bottomless pit that craves nearness, intimacy, affirmation, connection, significance, yet fears it is unable to receive it, and runs away from it. Receive a healing from a lack of bonding with your parent. Holy Spirit of Truth, I give you permission to clean out all the poison of wounded-ness that the soul has known for years." —Sylvia Gunther

A Part of Me Has Died

Kyloon, the survivor who has always led the way, has finally realized that leading the way is only killing the host, Karen. She loves her too much to hurt her anymore. She must step down in order for Karen to take care of herself.

Kyloon has brought Karen through hell and back twice now in Karen's life. Now she must let go because the journey is too much for the host's body. Karen must take care of her broken body by herself. She must embrace herself and love herself as she is. If not, Kyloon, will kill her by always pushing her.

Am I schizophrenic? No! I am just acutely aware of the three parts of my personality.

I must love my body, my host, in order to survive. How do you love something that is broken?

The image of my daughter's anorexic body comes running to the forefront of my mind. She must do the same on a daily basis—she runs miles. What will happen when running starts killing her body? That is where I am in life. I ran, but I ran from myself. I ran from my broken body until today.

In 2012, the OT specialist gave me a six-hour evaluation. In order to clearly explain to me my condition, she used visuals to show me what my problems were and how I needed to take care of them. She showed me a teapot.

During the day, my brain, the teapot, cannot maintain normal function due to sensory processing deficits, working memory problems, and perceptual reasoning deficits. My teapot runs out of water quickly and I often "fry" my brain. This leads to extreme fatigue, which I frequently feel at the end of the day. If I don't refuel as often as every fifteen minutes, I can hurt my brain. I was killing myself. This I knew.

This was the reason Kyloon stepped aside and made Karen walk through the doors of the neuropsychologist in December of 2012. That was the beginning of this journey of discovering who Karen is, deficits and all, and learning how I can honor her.

The brain specialist, who was fantastic, wanted me to carry around a notebook and write down items that people said to me that I needed to remember: my "working memory."

The specialist told me to do sensory exercises every fifteen minutes to refuel my brain. She said to continue on the exercise and diet routine that I was already on to maintain body function. The sensory exercises would refuel the brain that was being depleted by my sensory perception deficits. I always need balance to feel comfortable. If there is too much chaos around me, I cannot get my balance. That's why I have always avoided the malls and loud concerts. This is real and I must accept it.

She also wanted me to make a list on a white board and keep it posted in my house. The list would state all the things that kept me out of balance and those practices that maintained my balance. This would help others understand what made me feel uncomfortable and out of balance, ultimately frying my brain.

There is a picture she portrayed of me that helped me understand.

You are a solid house. Your roof and your values are extremely strong.

The wall, your habits and daily routines, again, are very strong.

However, the foundation of your house, which is made of stones, is quite faulty.
The foundation is where my performance is based.
My perceptual reasoning, sensory perception, and working memory all have problems with their performance.

What this all means is that when others look at my house, it is all in order. However, the reality is my foundation is faulty. The stones have deficits, which, when even one is taxed, makes me weak. When two are taxed, I start to burn the water in my teapot. When all three are being taxed and heavily used, my house shakes and I burn the teapot.

I have now set up a lifestyle that is taking care of many of these deficits. I did this by default. This is why I am so good with kids with disabilities—been there, done that kind of mentality. I know all the tricks of the trade to make them successful.

Finally, Karen the host, can take over. Kyloon can step down. Karen, the child is right here beside, Karen, the adult. Kyloon is alongside cheering. Karen is ready to step up on the podium and introduce herself.

Hi! My name is Karen. I was hit by a car in 1967 and was a miracle child. I should not be alive. I know that by the grace of God, I am here to tell my story of survival. My last journey is to love all of me, take care of what I have, and honor and respect every part of my being, broken or not. I believe by loving and honoring my body, soul, and mind, I can honor my Lord and Savior, all the greater. I can do it from a healed heart that I have been searching for all of my adult life.

"Lord, create in me a clean heart so that I may be of service to You."

A New Life as a Whole Person Begins

Now I am whole. Karen the child, Kyloon, and my true self have reunited and I can now start to teach my daughters how to respect themselves and others in a much healthier way. I can teach them not to allow unacceptable behaviors to happen to them because they feel they are not good enough. I no longer feel the constant underlying fear of rejection which truly affected me all the time, so I am free of that pain in the chest. I have noticed a childish part of my personality emerging who loves to dream. I remember her imagination and energy. Wow, God is good!

With the new me, I can begin working for God, hopefully with less baggage and a greater passion that will enable me to do an even greater job for Him. I want to follow God's lead on a minute-by-minute basis, letting Him take the lead, always living in the "Now." To do this, I must constantly keep my thoughts in check and aligned with God, and not on self or negative thoughts. As most of us know, this is not an easy task, but with God, all things are possible.

> *Jesus looked straight at them and answered, "This is impossible for human beings but not for God; everything is possible for God."* (Mark 10:27 GNT)

God Moments

Have you ever felt you just *knew* God had intervened in your life circumstances because the results were uncannily in your favor? Well, here are my God Moments, as I call them. I just want to share a few and hope that they will help you identify similar moments in your own life.

At first, I did not realize His hand on my life. Then I started to look back and see His hand of deliverance. Let me assure you, I needed many such moments.

As an eleven-year-old child, God saved me from a physical death.

- At nineteen years old, I gave my life to the Lord in the Canary Islands.

- At twenty-six years old, I was engaged to a Taiwanese man, who once I returned to the States to prepare for the wedding, mysteriously disappeared.
- At the age of forty-two, because I had been experiencing grand mal seizures at night during sleep since the age of eighteen, the doctors tried everything to control them with medication. Once, I was even scheduled for brain surgery. Their only solution was to keep giving me heavier medications. No longer able to function under such heavy medication, I walked into the principal's office of the school where I was working and tried to resign. The assistant principal, who was in the office at the time, proceeded to tell me, "That's not good enough." He told me that he had just attended a seminar on the brain and was going to send me to a specialist before he would let me quit. This specialist put me on a new medication; grand mal seizures stopped with no side effects.

Okay, at this point I knew God wanted me whole for some reason.

- At the age of fifty-two, I once again had a near-death experience. This time, I was emotionally and spiritually near death. But instead of a physical intervention, I actually heard a voice speak to me and say, "Change." This was the beginning of my journey to seek the process of cleansing my heart of all the garbage that had accumulated since childhood. Because of my obedience to His voice, this ultimately led to my journaling with God.
- At the age of fifty-seven, a good friend sent me an e-mail about writing transformational books. Because my friend was listening to God's voice to click that send tab to me, my book, *Clean Heart*, was written.
- At the age of fifty-eight, I took a big leap of faith, as God had been prompting me to do: **"go out and teach."** Well, at that time, I *was* a teacher, and I said to God, "But I'm already a teacher." His reply was, "Go out and teach." So, I

approached a friend and asked if I could teach a class for women using my manuscript for *Clean Heart.* This is how my ministry began.

- Today, I begin every day in prayer, early in the morning, with God. I ask Him daily, "What do You want me to do today?" Then I quietly wait for His reply.

I wish blessings for you, and I pray that you will learn how to listen to His voice, recognize when it is the Lord speaking, and act upon His instructions. The first step is to rid your heart of all the strongholds that bind you to your past. You, too, can and will have your own God Moments.

EPILOGUE

N ow, at the age of fifty-five, I have gained great insight, knowledge, and wisdom from my journey through divorce and forgiveness. The hardest and most difficult challenge was to forgive the many mistakes and weaknesses I possessed. My survivor counterpart, Kyloon, constantly reminds me that I must love myself unconditionally, at all times. The child within reminds me to love life to the fullest.

My journey has brought me to an understanding that my ex and I were both damaged as children, but attracted to each other's strengths as adults. Unbeknownst to us, as we fell in love and nurtured each other, the child in each of us would destroy the other. My deep need for love and affection could not be fulfilled by the damaged child of my husband. This need only brought out shame and frustration in my ex because he was not able to give me what I wanted most and needed. As a result of this frustration and inability to give love at such an emotional level, his natural response was to project anger at me. The child in me, who was extremely vulnerable, was not able to withstand his verbal threats and abuse. After many years of this type of behavior, we were caught in a verbally abusive relationship that neither of us was able to correct.

After years of therapy, and with God's patience, love, and direction, I am now able to continually seek refuge and healing in God's love. I continually seek His presence and advice, only longing to hear His small whisper. My desire is to help others and show them that there is hope for all.

Presently, I have wonderful relationships with both of my daughters, and a very friendly and amiable relationship with my ex. My oldest daughter has blossomed into a wise, loving, intelligent young woman. She is in constant communication with me, asking for Mom's advice and seeking Mom's counsel—much to my delight. My three-year-old grandson is the love of my existence. He is always welcome and allowed in my home whenever he and his mom are in town. My younger daughter has grown and matured into a beautiful, independent young woman with a strong sense of direction. She never ceases to amaze me with her social talents and abilities. She is a natural-born leader.

Wisdom Nuggets

"His strength shines best in our weakness. Jesus says to us, 'My grace is sufficient for you, for My power is made perfect in weakness.' Like Paul, we can say, 'I will boast all the more gladly about my weaknesses, so that Christ's power may rest on me.' That is why, for Christ's sake, I delight in weaknesses, in insults, in hardships, in persecutions, in difficulties. For when I am weak, then I am strong." (2 Corinthians 12:9–10)

Aren't you glad? It's called **grace**—God's enabling presence. "And God is able to make all grace abound to you, so that in all things at all times, having all that you need, you will abound in every good work" (2 Corinthians 9:8).

As Danny Silk wrote in his book, "Keep Your Love On," every relationship should be like a house. The foundation is constructed from Unconditional Love. From the foundation rises seven pillars. Love, Honor, Self-Control, Responsibility, Truth, Faith, and Vision. The roof covers the house with Peace, Hope, and Joy. The more you contemplate, meditate and digest the living Word in your heart, the more it will radiate in your life.

Questions to Ponder and Journal About

Read Romans 12:9-21 and write out all these verses on how to walk in His Spirit:

9–10: Love

11: Serving

12: Hope and perseverance

13: Hospitality

14: Bless those who persecute

15: One with one another

16: Humble yourself

17: Never pay evil for evil

18: Peace with *all* men

19: Let go, let God

20: Be kind to your enemy

21: Evil = good, good = love

I am so thankful that I decided to clean out my heart
and search for the truth rather than run.
Thank you, God, for cleaning out my heart,
so that I may hear Your voice and be of service to You.
Thank You, Lord, for loving me. —Karen, 2014

For a personal consultation on how Karen can help you, your loved ones, or your group, contact Karen at www.thepowerfulwomenofgod.org and please leave a brief description of your request or need. Messages will be answered within a few days. She honors each and every request with prayers while anticipating God's blessings on each.

REFERENCES

Al-Anon's Twelve Steps & Twelve Traditions. New York: Al-Anon Family Group Headquarters, 1981.

"Amen—AbeBooks." http://www.abebooks.com/servlet/SearchResults?an=amen; August 2, 2011.

Backus, William D., Ph.D. *The Healing Power of a Christian Mind: How Biblical Truth Can Keep You Healthy.* Minneapolis, MN: Bethany House, 1996.

Beattie, Melody. *Codependent No More: How to Stop Controlling Others and Start Caring for Yourself.* Center City, MN: Hazelden, 1992.

The Bible Promise Book: New International Version. Uhrichsville, OH: Barbour Publishing, 1990.

Evans, Patricia. *The Verbally Abusive Relationship: How to Recognize It and*

How to Respond. Holbrook, MA: Adams Media Corporation, 1996.

Holy Bible (New Revised Standard Version). London, England: Society for Promoting Christian Knowledge, 2008.

Katie, Byron, and Stephen Mitchell. *Loving What Is: Four Questions That Can Change Your Life.* New York: Three Rivers Press, 2002.

Meyer, Joyce. *Enjoying Where You Are on the Way to Where You Are Going: Learning How to Live a Joyful Spirit-led Life.* Tulsa, OK: Harrison House, 1996.

Moore, Beth. *Breaking Free: Making Liberty in Christ a Reality in Life.* Nashville, TN: LifeWay, 1999.

Podell, Ronald M., and Porter Shimer. *Contagious Emotions: Staying Well When Your Loved One Is Depressed.* New York: Pocket Books, 1992.

Prince, Joseph. http://www.josephprince.org/daily-grace/grace-inspirations/

Rosen, Laura Epstein, Ph.D., and Xavier Francisco Amador, Ph.D. *When Someone You Love Is Depressed: How to Help Your Loved One without Losing Yourself.* New York: Simon and Schuster, 1996.

Silk, Danny. *Keep Your Love On: Connection, Communication & Boundaries.* Redding, CA: Red Arrow Media, 2013.

Tolle, Eckhart. *A New Earth: Awakening to Your Life's Purpose.* London: Penguin, 2008.

_____. *The Power of Now: A Guide to Spiritual Enlightenment.* Novato, CA: New World Library, 1999.

Yancey, Philip. *Where Is God When It Hurts?* Grand Rapids, MI: Zondervan Publishing House, 1990.

CPSIA information can be obtained at www.ICGtesting.com
Printed in the USA
BVOW08s1811090716

454975BV00001B/2/P